MW00950771

Winter 2017

CHRISTIANITY**NEXT**

↓

Asian American Christianity
& Dones and Nones

Editor-In-Chief: Young Lee Hertig

Editorial Board: Edward Yang, Jessica ChenFeng, Mark Chung Hearn, Milton Eng
Advisory Board: Amos Yong, Kay Higuera Smith, Robert Romero

CHRISTIANITYNEXT

An interdisciplinary, scholarly exploration
of Asian North American Christianity

ChristianityNext is a journal of
Innovative Space for Asian American Christianity (ISAAC)

Membership subscriptions, address changes, advertising
and business correspondence should be sent to:
Innovative Space for Asian American Christianity (ISAAC)
4706 Via Colina #780, Los Angeles, CA 90042

Postmaster: Send address changes to:
ChristianityNext (ISAAC)
4706 Via Colina #780, Los Angeles, CA 90042

ISBN: 978-1-365-65421-3

Young Lee Hertig, Editor

Please send submission inquiries to *articles@christianitynext.org*

Cover and interior layout by Winnow+Glean

INNOVATIVE SPACE FOR ASIAN AMERICAN CHRISTIANITY (ISAAC)
4706 Via Colina #780
Los Angeles, CA 90042
http://isaacweb.org/christianitynext

Winter 2017

Asian American Christianity & Dones and Nones

Articles

Narrative Articles

Book Reviews

Russell Yee, Managing Editor of SANACS

A scholarly society with dues-paying members, regional meetings, an annual convention, book awards, a newsletter, and of course an academic journal—in late 2007 was our dream for the Society of Asian North American Christian Studies (SANACS). Timothy Tseng and I further dreamt this much-needed scholarly attention to Asian North American Christianity could span both evangelical and mainline; Protestant and Catholic; charismatic and non-charismatic; American and Canadian; East- Southeast- and South-Asian ancestries, and first- and later-generation viewpoints. In the years that followed, our sense of the need and the possibilities only deepened—but so did the hard realities of aspiring to so much with only volunteer efforts and no institutional home outside ISAAC (then a startup itself). The first edition of the journal came out in 2009. In the end we did produce four full blind-juried editions and one special issue of the SANACS Journal, for which we are thankful. We hope that ChristianityNext can build on this legacy and perhaps contribute to new and different approaches to the continuing needs that SANACS aspired to meet.

Young Lee Hertig

 is co-founder and Executive Director of Innovative Space for Asian American Christianity (ISAAC) and a founder of Asian American Women On Leadership (AAWOL). She has been teaching in the Global Studies and Sociology Department at Azusa Pacific University since 2002. She was formerly a Vera B. Blinn Associate Professor of World Christianity at United Theological Seminary in Dayton, Ohio (1998-2002), and an Assistant Professor of Cross Cultural Ministry at Fuller Theological Seminary (1992-1995). She is an ordained Presbyterian clergy and was a Commissioner of the Presbyterian Church USA to the National Council of Churches Faith and Order from 2002-2012.

Young Lee Hertig, Editor-in-Chief of ChristianityNext

ChristianityNext is an interdisciplinary, peer-reviewed journal for Asian North American Christian academics and practitioners. It affirms its evangelical and ecumenical roots and asks different questions and practices new ways of being. Its contribution is both theoretical and practical and it values both original research as well as lived experience. We welcome articles and book reviews for annually themed issues impacting Asian North American Christianity. We welcome contributions from published authors and first-time researchers in shaping our shared knowledge and consciousness for the Asian North American church and society.

In grappling with issues related to envisioning ChristianityNext, we seek to not only galvanize the voices but also be heard and incorporated both in academia and the church. For this mission, scholars/practitioners joined the Editorial staff, and Advisory Editorial board in 2016. Special kudos go to the blind jurors who read carefully the articles assigned, Eunice Ho, Administrative Assistant, and Alysha Kim, ISAAC's Research Fellow who proof-read all the articles.

The regional, generational, and economic divides in the United States have surfaced into broad daylight in the recent Presidential election and begs for face-to-face human engagement across differences. The sharp division between white evangelicals and evangelicals of color also was notable in this election. The demographic shift, the eclipsing power of Christendom in an age of "dones" and "nones," (those "done" with Christianity and those who check "none" in the religious affiliation box) and the backlash of globalization call forth reimagination of Protestant Christianity. This divided country is in greater need of engaging the Others, rather than alienating them. Therefore, more than ever, the mission of creating an innovative third space that embodies the radical love of Jesus that unites, rather than disunites, has become more imperative than ever. During vulnerable moments, people tend to opt for an extremism that often reverses collective progress. In this culture of privatization of public goods and the winner-takes-all style of economic inequity, Christianity's private faith must demonstrate a prophetic public witness. People of God are searching for a space that pursues something greater than their own private beliefs.

We boldly ask what it means to be the body of Christ in today's context. What is the Asian American call to this moment and beyond? The answers seem to lie in the problems themselves. With the rise of unchurched Millennials in the changing landscape from which they do church, the church as it is, needs to grapple rather than fear the situation. Today we imagine several answers from biblical truth and sociological contexts as follows:

1. Create a crucial, innovative space in the church. Often churches lack ears to hear but have abundance of lips to monologue.
2. Adapt an alternative Christianity that awakened the early church in Acts 2.
3. Address crucial but silent issues of the church such as enormous income inequality that allows 75 % of the economy to be hijacked by one percent in the United States.

At the heart of an innovative space is a pioneering spirit of courage, creativity, and risk. Innovation requires courage in the face of barriers and boundaries which are dynamic in nature, reminiscent of a mutating virus. Innovation also requires creativity to "think outside the box," to borrow the colloquialism, and to transgress those barriers and boundaries in unexpected ways. And because these unexpected ways preclude us from ascertaining our desired outcome, innovation inevitably asks us to don a posture that not only calculates risk but embraces it. In the face of increasing numbers of "dones" and "nones," among Asian Americans who reject Christianity, what posture is this and what answers does its subsequent innovation potentially offer us? In this journal authors, researchers, scholars, leaders, and thinkers alike not only delineate spiritual challenges ahead but also take upon themselves the task of pioneering innovative spaces for change.

In reimagining Christianity, the journal ChristianityNext takes an intersectional and interdisciplinary approach. As part of marking our 10th anniversary we have made two changes: 1) ISAAC now stands for Innovative Space for Asian American Christianity; 2) ChristianityNext replaces SANACS (Society of Asian North American Christian Studies). We are deeply committed to transcribing Asian American Christian contributions to the United States. The name ChristianityNext comes from ISAAC's 7th Symposium on February 27, 2016 that addressed "dones and nones," based on the Pew Research findings (symposium keynote address and panel presentations are available here: https://vimeo.com/channels/isaac7). The questions we addressed are listed below:

1. What factors contribute to the increasing number of "dones" and "nones" in the United States?
2. What cultural and sociological forces do Christian churches generally remain oblivious to?
3. What are some of the critiques of the church from "dones" and "nones"?
4. What internal structural barriers impede churches from adapting to shifting religious demographics?
5. What new forms of ecclesial expressions can we imagine?
6. What are the barriers blocking intergenerational/racial/gender/denominational dialogue?
7. What is the process for reimagining the Christian church?
8. What impact does "Black Lives Matter" have on the church?
9. What are practical steps for the revitalization of the church?

Richard J. Mouw, in his opening address stated that "dones" and "nones" are not for the most part atheist—many say they believe in God, even more are "spiritual," and yet are religiously unaffiliated. Quoting Robert Putnam, Mouw offered statistics regarding "dones" and "nones":

46% of Americans seldom or never pray before meals, 10% pray once or twice a week, and 44% pray at least daily. Mouw stressed, "America is divided now between grace-sayers and non-grace-sayers." Kay Higuera Smith, New Testament postcolonial scholar addressed all nine questions above. In response to the growing number of "dones" and "nones" she states,

In some ways the kind of evangelicalism characterized in largely Anglo-European communities is hoisted on its own petard. It has so successfully coopted the term "Christian" that many people who are drawn to Christ imagine that the only way that Christ is being worshipped communally is in our mega-churches. As our culture continues to be distrustful of unchecked power, people are just checking out.

One of the millennial attendees of the Symposium #7 exited from her particular ethnic church and shares why:

As a millennial who has been hurt by the Church, it can be easy to fall into the pattern of thinking that I am the only one in my situation. I know that God loves the church, so when my attitude towards the church is one of bitterness, I often wonder if that means that God is bitter towards me. The #ChristianityNext symposium provided me with a different perspective—it reminded me that God's love for me runs deep, even in the tension of trying to figure out where I stand with the Church. I am grateful to have had a space to process the pain that has accumulated through the years. I walked away from this year's symposium with a fresh sense of hope, and it has started me on the path towards healing and redemption."

-Janelle Paule

In responding to the cultural and sociological forces, Christian churches in general remain oblivious. Higuera Smith alerts us to adapt to radically changing cultural values of "radical individualism" and "the extreme collectivism of the traditional Christianity." At the core of evangelical collectivism resides fear of the social/cultural Other which we witnessed particularly in the last two years. The following lists other key factors Higuera Smith elaborated in her presentation:

- Deference to an authority figure
- A radical cultural tension between generations

- Lived morality and value clash
- Lack of Prophetic Witness
- Interrogating the collusion of power and money
- Call for prayer, collective repentance, and mediation

Russell Jeung uses qualitative interview methodology to dialogue with Chinese American millennials about their worldview and how they have come to ultimately reject the Christian church in lieu of personal sufficiency and familial loyalty, among other reasons. Jeung's article creates an intellectual space that may aid the Asian American church to not only better understand those who have declared themselves "done" with the church but also to have grace for them and exhibit Christ's love in a more relational manner.

Robert Romero reflects his own straddling of different identities and spaces as a Chino-Chicano (Chinese Chicano). In the spirit of Christian organizers and activists preceding him, Romero advocates for a space for Critical Race Theory in theological circles while acknowledging the dismissive attitudes from both camps that make this endeavor challenging. Using a storytelling, constructionist methodology, Jeney Park-Hearn centers second generation Korean Americans in her article "Prayers of Lament: Making Space for our Disenfranchised Grief" as she addresses the question of the second generation's burdensome legacy of unacknowledged grief interwoven into their inner landscape. She seeks an innovative space for the acknowledgment of pain to make way for healing. Clergywoman Ajung Sojwal writes in "The Impact of Recent Immigrant Women Ministers in the Church" about the racist and sexist barriers to electing Asian Americans (read: women of color) to positions on the clergy. In the spirit of inclusion, she hopes to encourage the church to take the faithful risk to appoint women of color to ecclesiastical leadership.

Finally, immigration, war, trauma, racism, postmodern ideology, and external factors are unquestionable realities that the church at large can choose to view either as hostile agents of destruction or as opportunities for faithful submission to a creative God who empowers us to better equip the church to embrace those who dare to raise questions and even critique the church as it is and reimagine where the church should be. The radical love of Jesus allows living out the upside-down, inside-out, and outside-in Kingdom of God here on earth. Reorienting complacency and breaking into the reign of God, indeed, is what we imagine. For these end, we boldly reimagine unity, not uniformity, of the body of Christ, and the public witness in the age of the "dones" and "nones."

↓

Articles

Dr. Russell Jeung

is professor of Asian American Studies at San Francisco State University. He's author of At Home in Exile: Finding Jesus Among My Ancestors and Refugee Neighbors, as well as other books on Asian Americans and religion.

Chinese American Millennials:
The Worldview of the Non-Religious
and Their Relationship to the Christian Church

By Russell Jeung

Well, [visiting church] actually re-confirmed my beliefs as an atheist. I went to their Bible studies and Sunday worship, and what they're saying just didn't make any sense to me. They say stuff like, "Jesus died for our sins so we should worship Him. He's a great man; He died for our sins." That just didn't ring any bells with me.

-Jonathan Hu, 30 year old Shoe Salesperson

In this statement, Jonathan Hu, a second generation Chinese American from Albany, California, expressed why he wouldn't join a Christian church or pursue its teachings. He attended church worship services and Bible studies, but the teachings didn't seem reasonable to him nor did the worship experiences resonate with him. He continued to explain, "There's just so many different ways to interpret the Bible. You can't just say you should just trust the Bible because there're so many different interpretations of the Bible. And I thought they were being kind of manipulative." Jonathan found it difficult to adopt one, single interpretation of the Bible as he employed a postmodern assumption about the subjective knowledge. Additionally, he resisted being manipulated or forced into accepting religious truths, beliefs or values. Similarly, second generation Chinese Americans who do not affiliate with any religion—also known as religious nones—agree with Jonathan in their assessments about the Christian church: 1) experiences at church didn't move or resonate with them; 2) they didn't need the social or spiritual benefits of the church; 3) the teachings of the church were too dogmatic and at times, judgmental; and 4) members of the church were too pushy, manipulative, or hypocritical.

Based on the 2012 Pew Research Center Asian American Survey and forty-three in-depth interviews with second generation Chinese Americans who are religious nones, this essay explains the value system of Chinese Americans and how they relate to American Christianity, especially in regards to the Chinese American church.[1] Second generation Chinese Americans whose families arrived after the 1965 Immigration Act, in general, hybridize both a Chinese values orientation and an American sensibility towards religion.[2] Unlike those from Western Judeo-Christian cultures who prioritize religious beliefs and belonging to specific churches, Chinese emphasize the morals, ritual practices, and responsibilities instilled by religions.[3] Consequently, they consider key values and relationships more important than orthodox beliefs or church membership. Additionally, as Chinese Americans become socialized and educated in American contexts, they adopt Western sensibilities of individualism, tolerance, and increasingly, anti-institutionalism. Like many of their fellow American millennials, they reject religion as an institution but want to maintain some spiritual values. Given these two broad cultural influences, Chinese American religious nones hold family as their highest value and make "family sacrifice" the central narrative by which they organize their lives.[4] While they embrace family, those in this study do not follow Christianity for precisely the reasons named by Jonathan.

———

1   The 2012 Pew Asian American Survey included phone interviews of 728 Chinese Americans. See the in-depth interviews of Chinese Americans is part of a larger research project to examine the worldviews, value and belief systems, and ethics of Chinese Americans

2   Immigrants born abroad are the first generation to the United States. Their offspring born in the United States constitute the second generation. This study examines the second generation in order to understand the adaptation process of Asian Americans and religious change.

3   See Jeung, Russell, Brett Esaki, and Alice Liu. "Redefining Religious Nones: Lessons from Chinese and Japanese American Young Adults." Religions 6, no. 3 (2015): 891-911.

4   Russell Jeung, "Second Generation Chinese Americans: The Familism of Religious Nones," in Chen, Carolyn, and Jeung, Russell. Sustaining Faith Traditions: Race, Ethnicity, and Religion among the Latino and Asian American Second Generation. New York: New York University Press, 2012.

The first part of this essay describes briefly the value system of Chinese American Millennials and how they prize family in some surprising ways. Second, it details the major reasons why Chinese American religious nones choose not to follow Christianity, with about one-third having negative attitudes towards the Christian church. Finally, it suggests recommendations about how the Church might respond to these trends and contextualize the faith to be more culturally relevant to this ethnic group.

The Liyi Tradition:
The Moral Boundary System of Chinese

The term, religion, was a Western concept introduced to China in the nineteenth century. Instead of understanding their relationship to gods, spirits, and ancestors in terms of orthodox beliefs and exclusive church affiliations, Chinese related to the supernatural, to metaphysics, and to ethics in a different manner. The theoretical concept, liyi, helps to identify and understand this difference in the Chinese moral universe. Li translates to ritual propriety. Chinese are less concerned about believing in religion than they are concerned about doing religion. Proper conduct of rituals, whether formal offerings or informal acts of hospitality and greeting, inculcates moral virtues. Yi means righteousness, especially in regards to one's relationships and responsibilities. Confucianists combined the two words to be foundational in their concept of "humanity," or what makes humans different from animals or barbarians. Ritual propriety (li) was the means by which righteousness (yi) could be practically and properly embodied in the concrete, while righteousness (yi) was necessary to guide the practices that constituted li. By promoting liyi, they established a moral system of rituals and responsibilities which defined who was righteous and virtuous. Confucianism, as well as other religious traditions in China, structured themselves around these key elements of what constitutes an appropriate, moral system.

For example, Confucianism highlights virtues that are dimensions to a good life: loyalty, filial piety, reciprocity, propriety, and benevolence. Instead of being concerned primarily with affecting the supernatural, Confucian

Analects suggested that rituals such as ancestor veneration were significant in how they instilled moral values. In the same way, Chinese Popular Religion (including practices related to supernatural beings, qi, and luck) does not necessarily require faith, belief, or correct truth knowledge, but more so orthodox practice of the rituals. Thus, many Chinese are religious and devout in their adherence to particular practices, such as Lunar New Year taboos or feng shui architectural arrangements, without being firm believers in the existence of supernatural forces or the efficacy of their own acts.

Utilizing the liyi concept does not mean that beliefs in ultimate truth claims or belonging to religious associations are irrelevant to Chinese. Rather, they simply are not as relevant to the Chinese worldview as moral virtues and relational responsibilities. In holding a liyi value system, therefore, one can include the use of multiple religious traditions and teachings. Consequently, many Chinese and Chinese Americans are hard-pressed to identify with one, single religious affiliation and may simply write "none" in surveys of religion.

Furthermore, use of the liyi concept is more appropriate in examining the worldview of Chinese Americans and quite possibly, American millennials, because it helps to highlight what's most significant in their own lived experiences. Growing up in a more religiously pluralistic society where institutions are often mistrusted, these two groups are skeptical about exclusive and abstract truth claims. Instead, they much more likely to find ultimate meaning and purpose in what they see as authentic and relational.

The Family Values of Chinese American Millennials

When asked about the top goal which they value, Chinese American young adults rate "being a good parent" above other goals seemingly more related to their stage in life, including "being successful in a high-paying career" or "having a successful marriage." This highest objective reflects the family orientation of Chinese Americans, who tend to prize family responsibilities above all else. After reviewing the results of the Pew Asian

American Survey, this section will detail some ways in which Chinese Americans live out these family values.

In the 2012 Pew Research Center Asian American Survey, 157 of the Chinese Americans (21.5%) were under 30 years of age. Religious nones constituted almost 2/3 of this population (65.6%), the most of any ethnic group in the United States. Those affiliated with nothing in particular (also known as spiritual but not religious) made up the largest proportion of this group at 36.3%, followed by agnostics (15.9%) and atheists (13.4%). Overall, Christians composed just 17.8% of the Chinese American young adult population. (see Figure 1)

FIGURE 1: YOUNG ADULT CHINESE AMERICANS
N=157

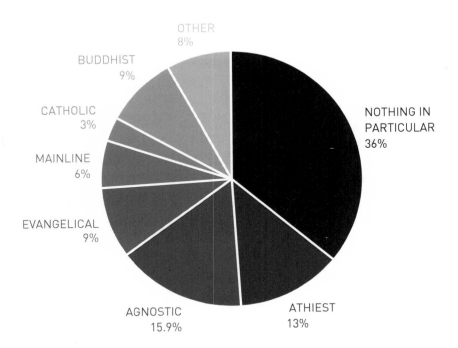

OTHER
8%

BUDDHIST
9%

CATHOLIC
3%

MAINLINE
6%

EVANGELICAL
9%

NOTHING IN
PARTICULAR
36%

AGNOSTIC
15.9%

ATHIEST
13%

Young Chinese American religious nones rate religion as less important to them than those who do affiliate with religion. Among Chinese Americans, only 19.0% of atheists and 15.8% of the nothing in particulars view religion as "somewhat important" to them and none said it was "very" important to them. Among all Chinese Americans, 20.6% said religions was "very" important and 25.1% said it was "somewhat" important. (See Figure 2)

FIGURE 2: IMPORTANCE OF RELIGION

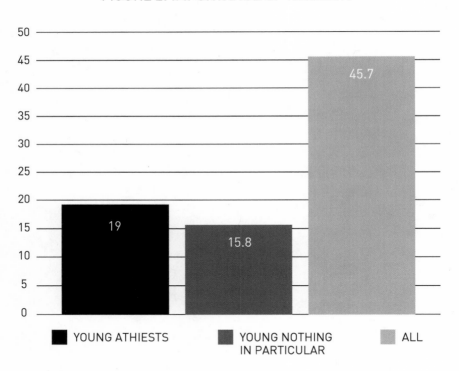

In terms of belief in God or universal spirit, religious nones varied again. Among Chinese American young adults, 43.9% of the nothing in particulars believed in God, but only 23.8% of atheists did, in contrast to the 63.5% of Chinese Americans overall who believed in God.

FIGURE 2: BELIEF IN GOD

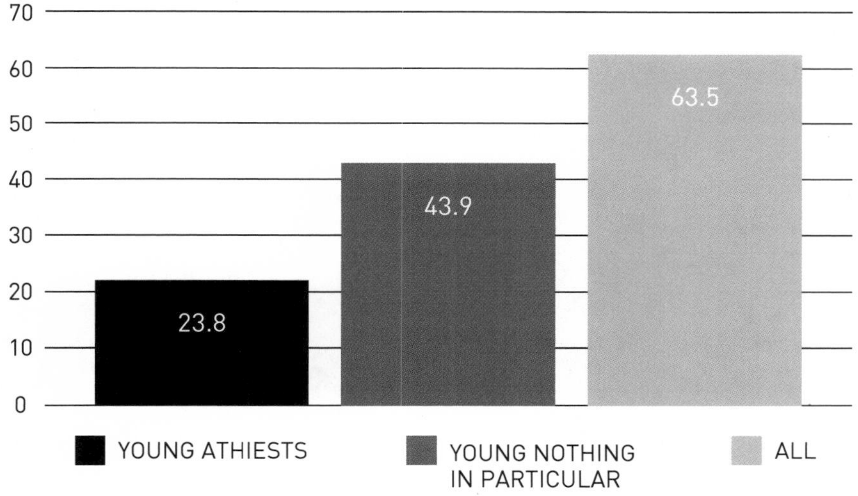

YOUNG ATHIESTS   YOUNG NOTHING IN PARTICULAR   ALL

Chinese American nones were more apt to believe in ancestral spirits than in God. One third of Chinese American atheists (33.3%) and 43.9% of nothing in particulars acknowledged that their deceased relatives continued to exist.

FIGURE 3: BELIEF IN ANCESTRAL SPIRITS

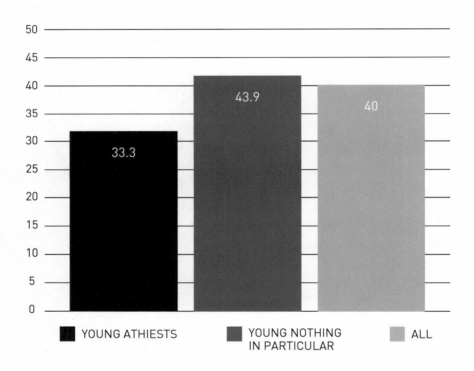

When asked about their most important goals, Chinese American young adults valued being good parents slightly higher than other Americans. Among Chinese Americans, 57.1% of atheists and 49.1% nothing in particulars rated this as their top life goals, as compared to 56.7% of Chinese American overall. In comparison, about half (52%) of American Millennials rated being a good parent as a top goal. (Figure 4)

FIGURE 4: BEING GOOD PARENTS

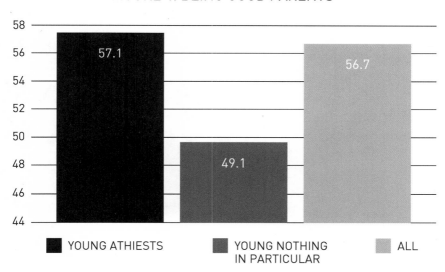

Having a successful marriage is the next highest rate goal, with 23.8% of Chinese American atheists and 43.9% of nothing in particulars citing this value. (Figure 5)

FIGURE 5: SUCCESSFUL MARRIAGE

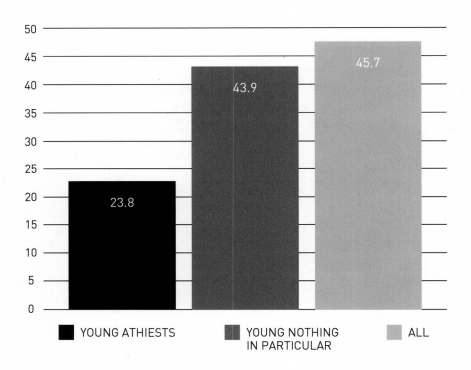

While young adults are at a stage in life to focus on their careers, career is not as an important goal for Asian Americans as their family lives. Only 9.5% of Chinese American atheists and 19.3% of nothing in particulars identified career as one of their top goals, as compared to 16.8% for all Chinese Americans. These percentages contradict the Model Minority stereotype, that Asian Americans are overachieving individuals who value their careers and work above all else. (Figure 6)

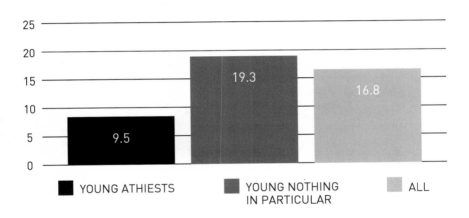

FIGURE 6: TOP GOAL - HIGH-PAYING CAREER

Another indicator of Chinese American family values is the role they believe that parents have in their lives. Chinese American young adults state that their parents should have some or a lot of influence in their careers and even marriage choice. In fact, 38.1% of atheists and 64.9% of nothing in particulars believe their parents should have some or a lot of say in their choice of careers. Overall, six out of ten Chinese Americans overall (62.9%) feel parents should have such career influence (Figure 7).

FIGURE 7: VALUES PARENTAL INFLUENCE ON CAREER

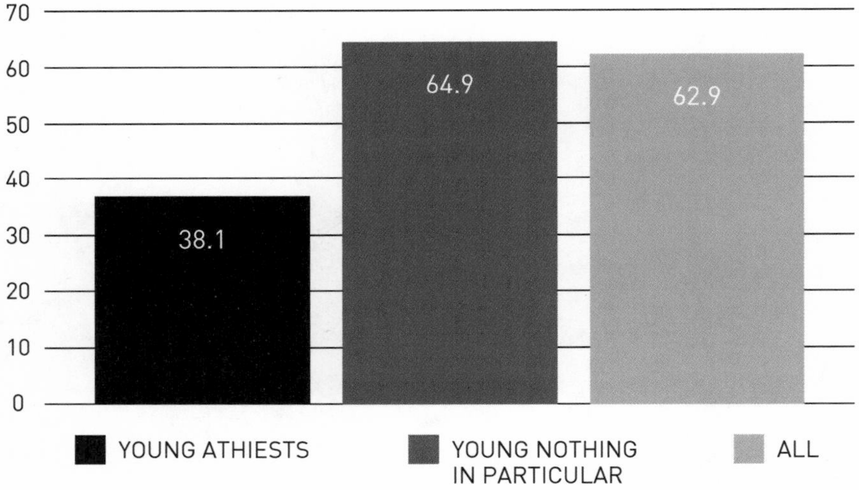

YOUNG ATHIESTS   YOUNG NOTHING IN PARTICULAR   ALL

Similarly, 42.9% of Chinese American atheists and 65.0% of nothing in particulars believe their parents deserve some influence in their choice of spouse, as compared to 56.8% of Chinese Americans who do. (Figure 8)

FIGURE 8: VALUES PARENTAL INFLUENCE ON CHOICE OF SPOUSE

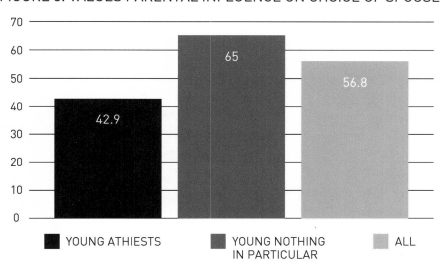

These values about the importance of family, especially of taking care of one's parents and being a good parent, are dominant themes in the in-depth interviews conducted with second generation Chinese Americans.[5] The great majority indicated that they are highly motivated by their immigrant parents' sacrifices for them, and they sought to honor those efforts. Several reported that they planned to have their parents live with them, and that they would quit their careers to relocate for their parents. Two anecdotes reflect the enormous importance placed upon caring for one's family.

---

5   While this national sample of 43 Chinese Americans is drawn from a non-random probability sample technique, it does indicate emerging trends and themes that are significant. 33 of these respondents made comments about the church and their trends are reflected in this essay.

Michael Chen, from San Francisco, grew up in a single parent household because his father abandoned the family when Michael was thirteen years old. The father racked up gambling debts, and then moved out after "womanizing." Yet when the father became aged and sick, Michael's mother encouraged him to take his father into his home and to care for him. He obeyed out of respect of his mother, even though he said he despised his father. The father then proceeded to get further into debt, and took out a second mortgage on the family home without informing the family. Even with this second, major act of betrayal, Michael again listened to his mother's plea to support their father. He summarized what his siblings think of their father: 'We're thinking about our family over ourselves by basically saying, "You know what, we're taking care of you because mom wants."'

Another Chinese American male, Larry So from Sacramento, California, also shared how he made his family a priority. He lent his cousin some money even at the disapproval of his fiancé, because he argued, "We always do stuff together, got each others' back. If they need help, you need to sacrifice your time." Although he was single, he reported that he was already saving money for his child's future education plans. And if he and his fiancé were to not have children of their own, he still planned to provide that savings for the future generation. He rationalized, "Even if we don't have a kid, I want to have [the savings] in case possibly another cousin's kid needs it. All of us have helped one another. I don't foresee it, but it's good to have a backup plan for the family or someone who has helped the family." Although these examples are extreme cases of family sacrifice, they do illustrate the extent to which Chinese Americans orient their actions and plans around their families.

Indeed, these Chinese Americans find that family is their primary source of identity and belonging. While other Americans may utilize religion, ethnicity, or profession for these personal and social needs, Chinese Americans rely on their family—both nuclear and extended—to give them meaning and purpose in life. Consequently, they may see less of a need for religious institutions compared to other Americans; their four main reasons for not pursuing Christianity are explained in the next section.

Factor #1
Religious Nones' Disconnect with God and the Church

The first reason that Chinese American young adults don't follow Jesus and join the church is that they did not connect with God through the Christian church. Over half of those responding about their relationship of the church (51.5%) made such comments. They stated they couldn't fully believe in Jesus Christ as God, they did not experience God at church, or they felt too out of place in the Christian context. As a result, they felt no desire to continue visiting churches.

One element of this factor is that the non-Christians didn't "believe" in God as they think religious followers ought to. The interviewees employed a Western "belief and belonging" model of religion, and could not embrace Jesus as the son of God. Irving Shue, who grew up in Scarsdale, New York, explored why the Christian faith was so important in others' lives. He explained, "I was curious that there's this thing—church—where so many people believed in it and it affected their lives so much. I was thinking, 'There's got to be something to religion that makes it so influential, so valuable to people.'" However, once he visited, he realized that it would be hypocritical for him to say he was a believer and he stopped attending: "When they told me I have to believe in it, or I was going to hell if I wasn't a Christian, it made me realize it was disingenuous for me to believe in this. So I stopped. But I enjoyed it. I didn't believe in this actual God, but they said I had to." In Irving's case, the clear-cut binary between belief and non-belief made him feel that he was being "disingenuous," even though he enjoyed going to church.

Whereas the first element of disconnect with God related to belief, the second element concerned with experience. Rhonda Woo, from Albany, a suburb of the San Francisco East Bay, was open and curious about church in high school, but was not moved at all while attending church a few times. She recounted,

> Yes, I was invited to church a few times, but it never appealed to me. I tried it out, but I couldn't get into the spirit, as they

called it. Well, I honestly found it really boring, and when they were reading off the Bible, I just couldn't focus. I'm not really sure why. Everyone there, they were really into it and saying the prayers, and they had a lot of emotion. And I couldn't do it. I think it's because I don't believe. They were like, "God will come to you, you will feel the Holy Spirit!"

Despite the exhortation of the church members and their own fervent worship, Rhonda could not explain why she did not feel anything: "I'm like, "Oh okay, I'll see what this is about." But I just felt like I just sat there, just staring at the wall or just on the floor when people were praying. Maybe I was being disrespectful, but I don't know." Although she tried to be open to God, Rhonda now affiliates as an atheist.

Similarly, Steph Wu, who was raised in Maryland, tried visiting her devout sister's church. Try as she might to pray to God like everyone else, she didn't have an earth-shaking, born-again conversion: "I've prayed; I'd bow my head for a second, then I'd open my eyes to see if anyone else is doing it. Everyone was really doing it, and it just felt weird. Obviously this isn't getting to me, it's not shaking my whole world like they think it's going to." Although the church members and her sister sought to convert her, she eventually distanced herself from them as she "felt less comfy hanging out with them."

Related to this disconnect with God was that six interviewees expressed how they "felt out of place" at church, because the setting and practices were too unfamiliar and foreign. Steph Wu continued to add that the alien nature of the white congregation she visited turned her off:

I went and felt really uncomfortable because we were the only people of color there. It felt really strange. I'd be shy around these people and they'd come up to me, and introduce themselves. They'd ask. "are you a member?" but I didn't know what it meant to be member of church.

Besides the demographics and Christian jargon, she didn't know how to read the Scriptures: "They'd give me the Bible and tell me what to turn to and everyone knew and I'd be flipping through the table of contents. Weird chapter verses--I didn't understand. At first I thought the chapters were alphabetical. They weren't. I just felt lost, really uncomfortable." Clearly, western churches, even in Chinese or Asian American congregations, were novel settings for young Chinese Americans that made them feel alien.

In summary, the majority of young Chinese Americans were open and curious about spiritual matters, but these religious nones found that they could not believe or experience God as Christians did. In their visits to church, church camps, and youth fellowships, they reported "nothing stood out;" "it didn't make much of an effect;" and "God didn't speak to me." They agreed that belief and faith ought to be authentic, so one respondent quit going to church because she "was pretending a little bit too much." These disconnects each deterred their further exploration of the Christian faith.

Factor #2
No Need for the Spiritual
or Social Benefits of the Church

Beyond not connecting with God through the Christian church, over one third of the sample (36.4%) expressed that they didn't feel the need for God or for the church.[6] Research on Asian American Christianity identifies how converts tend to join churches or fellowships initially for social or personal reasons, and how the church acts as a community and social service center.[7] However, these second generation Chinese Americans found that these needs were met elsewhere, especially through their own family networks.

Seven respondents stated that they recognized that the church was positive in that it offers a strong sense of community, but that they themselves

---

6   Respondents could cite more than one reason for not being Christian.

7   Chen, Carolyn. Getting Saved in America: Taiwanese Immigration and Religious Experience. Princeton, N.J.: Princeton University Press, 2008; Kim, Rebecca Y. God's New Whiz Kids?: Korean American Evangelicals on Campus. New York: New York University Press, 2006.

did not need that community. Leslie Dong from San Mateo, CA, agreed that church helps build a strong network, but noted that her family ties are enough for her. She explained,

> I actually think that going to church, aside from the religious aspect, seems like a good idea, because you have a sense of community, right? And it's social, and you have a regular thing where you interact with people and it seems great. And maybe I have enough of that with my own family, that we get together at least once a week.

Others also started attending church for social reasons, but realized that they needed to make stronger commitments to the faith if they were to continue going.

Besides not needing the social or personal benefits of the church, five interviewees stated that they felt no need for God. Benjamin Wong from the San Francisco Peninsula expressed point blank that he had no need for God, either for direction or for moral values:

> I don't think I need a God or I don't think I need a Bible to learn certain lessons, which is what I feel is the main point of religion. Or at least that's the best part of a religion, to have a guide, to teach you certain life lessons. But I never felt like I needed that to be a good person, to have morals, and to learn.

As an agnostic, he developed his own set of liyi values and ethics to live by.

In the same way, Jonathan Pan from San Mateo, CA, embraced an independent, self-sufficient attitude: "There are good things about church, it's just…philosophically just for me, I feel like I don't need it; I can make do on my own. As long as I believe in my own strength, my own willpower, hard work, and everything—I'm fine. I don't need it." Without any issues or crises pressing them to attend church, the respondents felt no need to seek a personal faith or to join a congregation.

Factor #3:
The Dogmatism of the Church

Along with not connecting to God and not needing the services provided by the church, the teachings of the Christian church were problematic for Chinese American religious nones. Almost one-third of the sample (30.3%) cited that they couldn't adhere to the teachings of Christianity because they were too dogmatic, strict, or anti-family. Since Millennials value tolerance, openness, and diversity, truth claims that are universal or morally clear-cut are challenged. This factor is a major explanation for why young Americans, as a whole, have increasingly left the church.

Karen Lai, from a Los Angeles suburb, describes how she wanted to maintain a range of beliefs but Christianity wouldn't allow her to do so. Although she could agree with aspects of the Christian message, she did not want to give up some other beliefs and values that she thought conflicted with it.

> When I was [at mass] this one Sunday, I was able to identify with everything they were saying. They would tell a Christian story, and this idea that you could reflect upon what that saint or person was doing. I would say, "Amen." I would understand the story and everything. But at the end of the day, when I go home, I don't feel like a bona fide Christian would say to me that I was part of their sect because I wouldn't necessarily want to abolish all my other beliefs that I have.

She felt that Christianity claims exclusive holds on the truth, and she couldn't commit to solely to this faith tradition.

Besides possessing exclusive truth claims, Christianity was also rejected because its moral teachings were seen as too strict. Rodney Shem, from another East Bay suburb, revealed, "I think I always knew I wanted to just not join any religion. because I thought it was too strict, too constricting. [My Mormon friend] would always tell me he felt guilty for watching rated R movies or watching porn." Three others similarly felt that religion shouldn't force moral strictures on individuals.

Finally, four respondents felt that the teachings of Christianity were not compatible with their family's beliefs and practices. Kenneth Lam, from Oakland, CA, shared a story about how he and his sister started attending church as children. When they tried to pray and thank God for their meal, the father erupted in anger. Kenneth recalled, "My dad worked his ass off to get the food, so he yelled, 'Why are you thanking God?' Maybe that's the reason why we stopped going to church." Thanking God instead of their father apparently was not very filial, so Kenneth and his sister had to quit attending church.

Further, Christianity has historically been rejected as a white man's religion, and a few respondents observed that their families did not approve it, so they also did not consider it. As Grace Chu from San Francisco succinctly put it, "My mom would say that Buddhism is better." Since these individuals could not agree with the teachings of Christianity, they consciously chose not to pursue this faith.

Factor #4
The Behavior of Christians

The last factor as to why Chinese American religious nones did not affiliate with the church was the behavior of the church members themselves. Nine interviewees (27.3%) commented that because Christians were too judgmental, pushy, or hypocritical, they were turned off by this religion.

Non-religious Chinese Americans claimed that Christianity was "too judgmental," especially when they were confronted with absolute truth claims or moral statements. Irene Hui, from San Jose, CA, especially was wary about established religion and its leadership. "I'm not very comfortable with the idea of established religion. I think it's gone to the point where it's really turned me off. Just the people, I feel, were being really judgmental; like if I didn't go to church one day, [they would question], 'Why aren't you going to church?'" Christians would rationalize that while

Christians may be judgmental, Christianity as a teaching taught grace and compassion. Irene retorted that the religion could not be separated from its leadership:

> [Christianity] is too judgmental. Reading the news, learning things about history, and being very aware of how corrupt the leaders of the institution is--not necessarily the people--but the leaders, I think I've gotten to the point in my life where I can't agree with that, and I can't support that, and it's almost a moral stance for me.

Like other Millennials, Irene could not tolerate the intolerance of the established church and its members.

In addition to disliking the perceived judgmentalism of Christians, Chinese American religious nones chafed against the pushy behavior of evangelistic Christians. They highly valued their freedom of choice and privacy, so being told what to believe was irritating and invasive. David Jong, who grew up in the Bible Belt in Amarillo, Texas, complained, "I had another friend who had a very abrasive way of pushing religion and that was definitely a turn off early on as well." Similarly, Laura Chan from Quincy, Massachusetts protested how Christians pressured her to become a fellow believer:

> I felt a lot of pressure; if you went [to youth group], they'd be like "Oh, okay, I didn't know you weren't [Christian] and then they give you that, "I feel sorry that you're not." I even had a Christian friend that said, "No offense, but you're going to hell." I said, "Okay, that's fine by me. Thanks for letting me know."

This pressure to believe, because of its eternal consequences of heaven or hell, was both too pushy and too judgmental for Laura.

Only one respondent critiqued Christians for being too hypocritical. Peter Hsieh, from Naperville, IL critiqued the Chinese church youth group where he was sent:

The same friends who would be in church crying, praying about how he needs to be a better person, would ask me to copy my homework at school. They were having sex. And this is like, I was in the mindset that, "Well, if this is real, if this is what you believe, then you know you should believe it." But it looks like no one really believes it, and there was just so much rampant hypocrisy. And it was a big turn-off.

Most respondents, however, noted the genuine faith and commitment of the Christians they knew.

Conclusion
Sociological Implications for the Asian American Church

The liyi mindset of Chinese Americans and their family value system have clear implications for the Church if it wants to reach out and minister to this community. First, presenting Christianity primarily as a set of doctrinal truths which require intellectual assent is a difficult task. Given the greater concern of Chinese Americans and American Millennials for authentic values and relationships, the Church needs—first and foremost-- to practice what it preaches and to embody grace, humility, love, and justice. Second, faith in Jesus does not necessarily have to entail clear-cut belief in absolute truth claims; individuals come to God with a range of questions. Instead, churches must make room for individuals whose faith includes following and obeying Jesus even with doubts—"Lord, help me overcome my unbelief!" [8] Third, Chinese Americans' concern for their families should be taken into account and supported. Non-churched parents might be more open to Christianity if it makes their children more honoring and respectful of their families.

Likewise, churches would do well to take into account the factors that deter religious nones from Christianity. To address individuals' disconnect from God and the church, leaders must recognize that this generation is

---

8   In Mark 9, Jesus heals a son whose father comes to Jesus with a mixture of belief and unbelief.

open to spiritual matters. Significantly, though, young Chinese Americans tend to "relate to" and "know" things experientially rather than just intellectually. While contriving situations where people meet God is off-putting, establishing sacred spaces where people might connect to Jesus and experience the Holy Spirit's movement—in a range of ways, settings and encounters—is critical.

The second barrier—whether or not religious nones recognize a need for God or for the Church—entails the Holy Spirit to convict people to repentance. Even so, this generation does see the need for social change and God's Kingdom of justice and peace.[9] To the extent the Church preaches and acts in the world to address these concerns, as part of Christ's message of salvation and redemption, it will be relevant.

Third, one's response to the perception that Christianity is too dogmatic depends on one's theology. Sociologically, churches with more absolute truth claims and moral standards grow, because they have higher demands on members. If people do choose a religion, they want one worth sacrificing for.[10] For those growing up in postmodern contexts, however, dogmatic statements are an anathema. Framing Christianity as a story by which one can journey through life, as a way (tao) to follow, or as a life-giving relationship with God are more resonant with this generation.[11]

Finally, Christians have the most control over how they themselves behave and relate to non-Christians. Gauging another's interest in spiritual concerns is a delicate matter. For each religious none who complained that Christians were too pushy, another said that Christians were not pushy. Since they were not invited to church or fellowship, they didn't attend. Ultimately, though, Christian hospitality, generosity and unity are virtues to be nurtured as we give others the space to explore the faith.[12] Similarly,

---

9   This Millennial generation has higher rates of activism, commitment to engaging their community, and helping others than ever before. See Cooperative Institutional Research Program, "The American Freshman: National Norms for Fall 2015," (Los Angeles, CA; Higher Education Research Institute, 2015).

10   Laurence Iannaccone "Why Strict Churches Are Strong." American Journal of Sociology 99, no. 5 (1994): 1180-211.

11   Christianity matches each of these framings. See John 14:6: "Jesus answered, "I am the way and the truth and the life. No one comes to the Father except through me."

12   See Hebrews 13.

statements about one's moral stances may be perceived as judgmental no matter how one tries not be arrogant or self-righteous. Despite the danger of gaining this reputation, Christians must continue to be prophetic and evangelistic voices in our society. If we speak the truth in love—with a major emphasis on the love—and live as consistently as we can to Jesus' ways, then perhaps we can be the witness of God's good news to which we are called.

Therefore, for the Asian American Church to contextualize the gospel for Millennials and religious nones, it must recognize their worldview that prioritizes values of authenticity, tolerance, and social justice over beliefs that are dogmatic. In demonstrating Jesus' way of love and hope that is countercultural to the American empire's power dynamics and inequalities, the Church can offer a prophetic witness and become a force of social change. And by being a family of God that includes all, it can build upon the Chinese American family values which are already prized among this group.

Dr. Robert Romero

 is an Associate Professor of Chicana/o Studies and Asian American Studies at UCLA. His book, The Chinese in Mexico, 1882-1940, received the Latina/o Section Book Award.

Towards a Perspective of the Christian-Ethnic Studies Borderlands and Critical Race Theory in Christianity

By Robert Romero

I am a Chinese-Mexican, Jesus-loving, pastor, lawyer, and professor of Chicana/o Studies and Asian American Studies at UCLA. My various cultural, spiritual, and academic intersectionalities collided and exploded like a multiracial supernova at the recent Latina/o Consultation hosted by InterVarsity Press. As part of this noteworthy event held in Chicago, nineteen Latina/o academics and ministry practitioners gathered from across the country to discuss the state of Latino Christian publishing in the United States. In the opening session we did an icebreaker. The question was asked: "Tell us something unique about yourself." Since I was a guest at an InterVarsity event, I tried to find common ground by stating, "My Chinese grandfather founded InterVarsity in China in the 1930s." A few minutes later at the next break I was approached by IVP editor Dan Reid, who asked, "Was your grandfather Calvin Chao?" Much to my surprise, God had in store a reunion that was sixty-seven years in the making.

I had heard the story a thousand times. As a young man in China in the 1920s, my Chinese grandfather Calvin Chao contracted the then deadly disease of tuberculosis. Presbyterian missionaries Sophie and James Graham nursed my grandfather back to health in their living room over the course of many months and saved his life. In loving remembrance, my grandparents named two of their children after them. Through the extravagant love and biblical hospitality shown him by the Graham family, my "Gung-Gung" came to know the love of Christ and was later used by God to found InterVarsity Christian Fellowship in China. He also authored influential Chinese-language theological texts, founded several seminaries in

Southeast Asia and the United States, and was dubbed "the Billy Graham of China" by Christianity Today magazine.

Sixty-seven years after these pivotal events in the living room of the Grahams, I had the privilege of meeting their great grandson, Dan Reid, at the Latino/a Consultation at InterVarsity Press in Chicago. Ironically, this gathering had nothing directly to do with China, Asia, or the Asian American community. We didn't plan this reunion, and we never knew each other before. As far as I know, our two families have not interacted for at least several decades.

Following our profound reunion, I went back to my hotel room in awe. I thought to myself, "Were it not for the love of Dan's great grandparents, I literally would not exist. What is God trying to tell me?" I then called my mom and she reinforced the significance of what transpired. She told me that my Gung-Gung considered Sophie Graham to be his spiritual mother and that Sophie Graham once told my grandfather, "If you were the only person who came to know Christ as a result of my many years of missionary work in China, it would have been worth it."

Shortly after this transformative experience in Chicago, I was graciously invited to write this essay for ChristianityNext. The task—construct a personal narrative and reflection which speaks to my multiracial experience in the church and academy, and which might be of practical application to the rising generation of millennials in the United States. After much musing and deliberation, I settled on the following questions for examination: (1) How does my intersectional cultural and spiritual experience reflect the broader experience of millennial Asian Americans, and other Christians of Color in the United States? How might our experience of alienation in the church and academy be conceived in terms of the metaphor of a "spiritual borderlands"? (2) As a practical response to the spiritual borderlands of institutional Christianity and Ethnic Studies, how might we frame a multidisciplinary, racially-focused, theological project which is relevant to the collective experience of the rising millennial generation? Drawing upon personal narratives, critical race counterstories, and "testimonios," this essay argues for the creation of a formal research project which may be called Critical Race Theory in Christianity.

The "Spiritual Borderlands" of Ethnic Studies and Institutional Christianity

As a professor of Chicana/o Studies and Asian American Studies, I straddle two ethnically distinct academic communities. I was once told by a colleague in Chicana/o Studies, "Some students of this department don't like you because you are half-Chinese, some don't like you because you are a Christian, and some don't like you because your wife is white." Though painful to hear, this comment was true. And, it helped explain the animosity I experienced on the part of a small, but vocal contingency of students who sought to challenge my prospects for tenure at UCLA.

Notwithstanding the challenge I received during the tenure process by this small group of student detractors, Chicana/o Studies and Asian American Studies are both good intellectual homes for me. For the most part, I am strongly supported by my colleagues and students with respect to my research in racial history and theory. My interdisciplinary research project of "Chino-Chicano," or "Asian-Latino Studies," has been strongly received by my colleagues in both home departments and respective fields of study. As a "Chino-Chicano," whose parents hail from Chihuahua, Mexico and Hubei in Central China, I have come along and argued that the definition of "Chicano" must be broadened beyond the dichotomy of Spanish and indigenous to include the rich contributions of Asians to Mexican history, culture, and tradition. Chinese, Japanese, and other Asian groups have been meaningfully present in Mexico and Latin America since colonial times, and in the early twentieth century, Chinese immigrants were the second largest foreign ethnic community in all of Mexico. Quite sadly, they were also the victims of a virulent Sinophobic campaign which culminated in the expulsion of most Chinese from the country in 1931. In light of this important history, I argue, we must incorporate the Chinese and other Asian communities into our understanding of Latino racial formation or "mestizaje." Almost without exception, my project of "Asian-Latino Studies" has been favorably received.

As a professor, my greatest sense of alienation, however, has arisen from the sometimes subtle, and sometimes outright, rejection of Christianity by the fields of Chicana/o Studies, Asian American Studies, and Ethnic Studies in general. Along with many other professors and students of faith, I have lived much of my academic life in the "spiritual borderlands" of the academy and institutional religion.[1] In the world of Ethnic Studies and activism our faith is usually discouraged or criticized. We are told, "You can't be a Christian and care about issues of racial and gender justice. It's the white man's religion and it's a tool of colonization. It's racist, classist, and sexist." As a result of such hostility, many Students of Color keep silent about their faith in activist circles for fear of persecution or ostracization. Others lose their faith. Some tenuously cling to a personal relationship with God but abandon institutionalized Christianity altogether.

This negative perspective of religion within Ethnic Studies is understandable. It is grounded in centuries of historical and contemporary misrepresentation of the teachings of Jesus. In a very real sense, the history of People of Color in the Americas is one of systemic racism perpetuated by white individuals claiming to be Christian. From the Native American genocide, to slavery and Jim Crow segregation, to Operation Wetback and the Asian Exclusion Laws, to the present day Tea Party movement, many individuals continue to perpetuate the stereotype that Christianity is a racist, classist, and sexist religion. And so, understandably, the world of Ethnic Studies continues to reject Christianity as part of its intellectual platform.

As a consequence of the wholesale rejection of Christianity in Ethnic Studies, many students fall away from their faith, as well as experience severe emotional damage. This grave consequence should cause us to take serious pause and is exemplified by the following critical race counterstory:[2]

---

1   The concept of "in between," "borderlands" identity was developed in Chicana/o Studies through the writings of Gloria Anzaldúa in her famous book, Borderlands/La Frontera: The New Mestiza (San Francisco: Aunt Lute Books, 2012).

2   As described by Solórzano and Yosso, critical race counterstories "draw on various forms of 'data' to recount the racialized, sexualized, and classed experiences of people of color. Such counterstories may offer both biographical and autobiographical analyses because the authors create composite characters and create them in social, historical, and political situations to discuss racism, sexism, classism, and other forms of subordination." Daniel Solórzano and Tara Yosso, "Critical Race Methodology: Counter-Storytelling As An Analytical Framework for Education Research," Qualitative Inquiry, Volume 8, Issue 1 (2002), 23-44; 33. The following counterstory of "Rosa" is based upon the life experience of a student I met three years ago at a Christian social justice event in Pico Union.

Rosa was excited about attending her first college lecture. She was the first of her family to attend college and was the valedictorian of Roosevelt High School. Her 4.2 grade point average had earned her a full ride to Pitzer College, one of the best liberal arts college in the U.S. according to U.S. News and World Report.

Rosa's Mom and Dad were deacons in their local church and had brought her up to be a Christian. They told many stories of how God had taken care of them when they made the dangerous journey to the United States across the Sonoran desert. Her dad worked two jobs—as a short order cook during the week and a gardener during the weekend. He also collected cardboard to raise extra money for the family. Her mom was a nanny to a rich family in San Marino and also managed their family of four kids. Church provided one of the few spaces of social respect for Rosa's parents. They had "dignidad" when they walked into church and were addressed as "deacons," and "hermano" and "hermana" Ramos.

Rosa's first class was a Chicano history class, and her professor began his lecture by saying, "Christianity is the White Man's religion." The professor went on to detail how the Spaniards used Christianity to colonize the Aztecs and the millions of indigenous people of the Americas. Rosa also learned about how the Bible was used to justify ethnic genocide, murder, and the oppression of women. Rosa left class devastated. She didn't know what to do. Who was right about Christianity? Was it her working class, immigrant parents who loved and followed Jesus? Or was it her professor who had his Ph.D. from Harvard and had written many famous books over the past twenty years?

When I met Rosa she was in her second year of college and undergoing clinical depression. Rosa had been seeing a psychiatrist to help her with the deep loss and emotional conflict she was experiencing trying to reconcile the faith of her youth with the perspectives of Christianity she had learned in her classes.

In addition to creating deep emotional turmoil for many students like Rosa, another consequence of the wholesale rejection of Christianity by Ethnic Studies is that thousands of potential students are unnecessarily turned away from disciplines such as Chicana/o Studies, Asian American Studies, and African American Studies. If asked to choose between the faith of their family and Ethnic Studies, they reject Ethnic Studies. I can understand this decision, and it keeps thousands of students of color from coming to study Ethnic Studies at the university.

The flipside of the spiritual borderlands experienced by activist professors and students of faith is the strong sense of alienation we feel in some institutional religious spaces. We often feel out of place in church, seminary, and parachurch ministry circles because our strong concern for racial justice is not understood. When we share our concerns about issues of educational inequality or the need for compassionate immigration reform, we are met with blank stares or even outright opposition. We are told, "Those are political issues which are separate from faith." "How can you be a Christian and not support the Republican candidate?" As a result, we often walk away from church and formal religious institutions. We may cling tenuously to a personal faith, but our activism becomes divorced from institutional Christianity.

This unfortunate spiritual alienation is illustrated by the counterstory of Paul. Paul grew up in Korean Christian circles and entered UCLA with a meaningful personal faith. As an Asian American Studies major, he learned about the historic injustices faced by Asians and Pacific Islanders in the United States. He learned about things like the Chinese Exclusion laws which barred Chinese immigrant laborers from the United States from 1882-1943, the Alien Land Laws which took away the right of Japanese immigrants to own property in California, and the internment of Japanese Americans during WWII. His social consciousness was especially raised during a study abroad trip to Hawaii where he learned about the immoral conquest and colonization of Hawaii. After returning, John searched to find other Asian American Christians who understood these issues and who were committed to the struggle for social change. He found none. As a consequence, he walked away from church, holding tenuously to his personal faith in God.

Two recent examples from my own life are also illustrative of the alienation which many Christians of Color experience in institutional religious spaces. As a pastor, professor, and immigration lawyer, I am passionate about comprehensive immigration reform. Seeing that my local church was not doing much in this area, I wrote and told them, "Immigration is the cutting civil rights issue of our time. It's like slavery of our day. Why isn't our church doing anything about this?" In response, I had a meeting with the pastor to explain my concerns. Unfortunately, I was met with defensiveness and pushback. I left devastated. I felt discombobulated for days. To soothe myself on my drive to UCLA the next day, all I could do was blare Latino music in my car and allow the beats, rhythms, and melodies of my culture to comfort me and overwhelm my senses. I thought to myself, "My Brown skin and Latino-ness is welcome to improve the superficial appearance of diversity in the pews, but my viewpoints and perspectives which flow from my Brown experience are not welcome. They want me to be Brown on the outside, but White on the inside. My Latino-ness was not truly welcome. I could not attend this church and be Asian-Latino." I left the congregation in search of a church where my Asian-Latino cultural heritage was truly welcome.[3] Much to his/her credit, the pastor eventually apologized to me. I was not, however, invited to contribute to further discussions on the topic of immigration. Two years later, the invitation came.

Story two. In 1997 as a third-year law student at Berkeley School of Law, I received my call from God to become a professor. The vision: complete law school, pursue a Ph.D. in Latin American history, and as a professor, speak and write about issues of race and ethnicity. Instrumental to my calling was a talk I heard by noted Christian speaker Os Guinness at a parachurch ministry event in 1997. Flash forward a decade. I'm a professor at UCLA and this same parachurch ministry comes to campus and gets wind of my story. They ask me to moderate an event featuring Os Guinness. Since I was sincerely grateful for the role played by their ministry in my life, I agreed to serve as moderator and to allow my story to be featured in their newsletter. Fast forward a few more years. I decide to write my first Christian book, Jesus for Revolutionaries: An Introduction to Race, Social Justice, and Christianity.[4] The idea behind Jesus for Revolutionaries was

---

3   Thankfully, I found such a church in La Fuente Ministries in Pasadena. La Fuente is a liberationist, evangelical church headed by Marcos and Andrea Canales.

4   Robert Chao Romero, Jesus for Revolutionaries: An Introduction to Race, Social Justice, and Christianity (Los Angeles: Christian Ethnic Studies Press, 2013). A free e-book copy of Jesus for Revolutionaries may be accessed at: http://www.jesusforrevolutionaries.org.

simple: Write a book, in conversational style, which would provide a biblical, historical, and sociological introduction of Christianity to activists. As another important goal, the book would introduce readers to the little-known world of Christian community development and social justice.

Excited about the close relationship I had recently forged with the aforementioned para-church ministry, I decided to float my book manuscript to them for potential publication. What a potentially good fit, I thought. They had played such a meaningful role in my life, they have a book series featuring professors, and one of their main goals was to foster engagement with the academy. In addition, social justice was an explicit topic featured on their website. Enthusiastically, I presented my book manuscript to them. One month later, I received a polite rejection: "Our book series is small and we're publishing only on a limited number of topics at this time. Unfortunately, yours does not fit in." I was devastated and deeply angered.

I thought to myself, "So it's ok to use me as a diverse, Chinese-Mexican poster boy for fundraising, but when I seek to publish a book about all that God has taught me about race and social justice since being touched by your ministry, the answer is no? What else could I do to make myself qualified to publish a Christian book? I have two doctorates, one from Berkeley and one from UCLA. I am a tenured-track professor of Chicana/o Studies and Asian American Studies at UCLA. I'm a lawyer. I'm a pastor. I've ministered to activist students throughout the country for a number of years now. What else could I do?" As we say in Spanish, ni modo.

After this disheartening experience, I tried, once again unsuccessfully, to float Jesus for Revolutionaries by another Christian publisher. I felt good about it. One week after submitting my manuscript to them, my first book, The Chinese in Mexico, 1882-1940, won a national book award.[5] About one week after that, I received tenure at UCLA. I was sure to let the publisher know about all these special events that had occurred in my life and academic career. Guess what happened? I never heard back. I was rejected again.

---

5   Robert Chao Romero, The Chinese in Mexico, 1882-1940 (Tucson: University of Arizona Press, 2010).

These rejections caused me to pray and reflect. How did God want me to proceed? What was my next course of action? My conclusion: God wanted me to self-publish Jesus for Revolutionaries so that I could make it available for free. After all, Students of Color do not have much money and often have to choose between buying school books and eating. They work multiple jobs and struggle valiantly to cover the basic expenses of their education.How could I ask them to pay $25 for a book called, Jesus for Revolutionaries? That would be deeply hypocritical. And so, I self-published the book under the imprint, "Christian Ethnic Studies Press." I offered Jesus for Revolutionaries as a free e-book and a low-cost paperback. I decided to donate 100% of the book proceeds towards scholarships for undocumented students and the operating expenses of our non-profit organization, also called Jesus for Revolutionaries.

These are just two stories among many I could tell. I believe they clearly demonstrate the predicament faced by many of us as Christian professors and Christian Students of Color. Although many Christian churches, universities, seminaries, and publishers claim to care about issues of race and justice, most are not willing to go beyond a superficial level of engagement. They are not willing to give voice to the actual stakeholders of social justice controversies, perhaps a token voice here or a token voice there. For the most part, however, they are not willing to "to go there." Push back and closed doors usually come when we professors and Students of Color speak frankly about our experiences of discrimination and racial injustice. The end result is the further spiritual and intellectual alienation of thousands of Christian students and academics of color.

Towards a Perspective of Critical Race Theory in Christianity

As a practical response to the spiritual borderlands of institutional Christianity and Ethnic Studies, I propose a new academic project—that of Critical Race Theory in Christianity. To those who may be unfamiliar, Critical Race Theory (CRT) examines the intersection of race, racism, and U.S. law and policy. In other words, it looks at how U.S. laws and public policy have been manipulated and constructed over the years to preserve privilege for those considered "white" at the expense of People of Color. For example, how did racism infect U.S. law and policy through slavery and Jim Crow segregation, and how does racism continue to cripple our legal, educational, political, corporate, and public health institutions? According to Richard Delgado and Jean Stefancic:

> The critical race theory movement is a collection of activists and scholars interested in studying and transforming the relationship among race, racism, and power. The movement considers many of the same issues that conventional civil rights and ethnic studies discourses take up, but places them in a broader perspective that includes economics, history, context, group- and self-interest, and even feelings and the unconscious. Unlike traditional civil rights, which stresses incrementalism and step-by-step progress, Critical Race Theory questions the very foundations of the liberal order, including equality theory, legal reasoning, Enlightenment rationalism, and neutral principles of constitutional law.[6]

Derrick Bell, Richard Delgado, and Alan Freeman were among the early progenitors of CRT, and the field has been developed in subsequent years by law professors Kimberle Crenshaw, Angela Harris, Ian Haney Lopez, Mari Matsuda, Kevin Johnson, Laura Gómez, and Cheryl Harris. [7] CRT has continued to build as a burgeoning intellectual movement, and it has spawned offshoots within education, sociology, political science, and Ethnic Studies. Quite conspicuously, a formal movement of Critical Race Theory has not emerged within the realm of theology, though postcolonial theology may be considered a close second cousin.[8]

---

6   Richard Delgado and Jean Stefancic, Critical Race Theory: An Introduction (New York: New York University Press, 2012), 3.

7   Ibid., 4-6.

8   For an introduction to postcolonial theology, see, Evangelical Postcolonial Conversations Global Awakenings in Theology and Praxis, eds. Kay Higuera Smith, Jayachitra Lalitha, L. Daniel Hawk (Downers Grove: InterVarsity Press Academic, 2014).

CRT has much to offer theological studies in terms of its incisive observations about the operation of race in U.S. legal history and policy. According to Delgado and Stefancic, the basic tenets of CRT include the following: (1) Racism is ordinary: "Racism is ordinary, not aberrational—'normal science,' the normal way society does business, the common, everyday experience of most people of color in this country."[9] (2) Interest convergence or material determinism: "Because racism advances the interests of both white elites (materially) and working-class Caucasians (psychically), large segments of society have little incentive to eradicate it."[10] (3) The Social Construction Thesis: "[R]ace and races are products of social thought and relations. Not objective, inherent, or fixed, they correspond to no biological or genetic reality…"[11] (4) Voice of Color Thesis: "[B]ecause of their different histories and experiences with oppression, black, American Indian, Asian, and Latina/o writers and thinkers may be able to communicate to their white counterparts matters that the whites are unlikely to know."[12] Beyond these basic tenets, other central themes of CRT include intersectionality, legal indeterminacy, white privilege, whiteness as property, revisionist history, and legal storytelling.[13] Although scholars of religion have much to learn from the rich ruminations of Critical Race Theory, I believe that the disciplines of theology and religious studies also have unique insights to offer.

In her classic article, "Whiteness as Property," Cheryl Harris persuasively argues that "whiteness" developed as a legal property interest in U.S. history and served as the basis for the inequitable distribution of socioeconomic and political benefits.[14] Those who possessed "whiteness" in the eyes of the law were viewed as full human beings and were entitled to citizenship, the right to vote, property ownership, etc. On the other hand,

---

9   Ibid., 7.

10   Ibid.,8.

11   Ibid.,8.

12   Ibid.,10.

13   Ibid.,5,10, 24-25, 84, 87-89.

14   Cheryl Harris, "Whiteness as Property," in Critical Race Theory: The Key Writings that Formed the Movement, eds. K. Crenshaw, N. Gotanda., G. Peller, and K. Thomas (New York: The New Press, 1995), 276-291.

those excluded from the possession of whiteness by the courts were legally defined as "black" and viewed as chattel. According to Harris, "Slavery as a system of property facilitated the merger of white identity and property.... Whiteness was the characteristic, the attribute, the property of free human beings."[15]

To build upon Harris' analysis, one might also say that British and other European imperial powers misappropriated Christianity as an aspect of their legal property interest in whiteness. In their view, Christianity was their property, and to be Christian was to be white. They alone held the institutional and theological keys to the Kingdom of God, and that justified their colonial expansion over Africa, Asia, the Americas, and the Near East. According to the Doctrine of Discovery, Europeans could violently seize the lands of non-Christian ethnic groups of the world for purposes of religious conversion.[16] Indeed, People of Color throughout the globe were considered "fortunate" to receive salvation of their souls in exchange for the small price of their lands and temporal slavery.

From the springboard of the Doctrine of Discovery surfaced a slate of perverted religious doctrines used to justify European colonial expansion well into the twentieth century. These far-fetched theological doctrines included syncretistic Aristotelian notions of "natural slavery," Manifest Destiny, mark of Cain theology, segregationist tower of Babel theology, and the manipulation of Kuyperian notions of sphere sovereignty to justify South African apartheid. At the core of all these twisted theologies was the implicit belief that Christianity belonged fundamentally to Europeans and their colonial descendants. As a consequence, the institutions of Christianity—individual congregations, denominational hierarchies, schools of theological education, and theology-- were their property as well. In exchange for the proclamation of a Eurocentric gospel and the salvation of colored souls they could rule both Heaven and Earth—so they thought.

Today, very few would make the bold claim that Christianity is the

---

15   Ibid., 279.

16   For an elaborate analysis of the Doctrine of Discovery and Manifest Destiny, see Robert J. Miller, "The Doctrine of Discovery in American Indian Law," Idaho Law Review 42 (2005-2006): 1-122; Miller, "American Indians, The Doctrine of Discovery, and Manifest Destiny," Wyoming Law Review 11 (2011): 329-349.

property of whites alone. After all, Christianity is on the decline in Europe and among whites in America.[17] Moreover, the Christian faith is experiencing rapid growth in Latin America, Asia, and Africa, and holding strong among Latinos, African Americans, and Asian Americans in the United States.[18] The non-white numerical trajectory of global Christianity is not contested. At the same time, however, the institutional structures of Christianity in the United States remain firmly white.[19] As in earlier times of de jure segregation, white male leadership continues to dominate over individual congregations, religious denominations, publishing houses, seminaries, and Christian colleges and universities. I do not doubt that the vast majority of these leaders possess good will and in true sincerity do not harbor explicit racism. Some, in fact, hold a profound sense of racial consciousness and are aware of their white privilege. For many, however, their limited cultural lens does not allow them to see that the institutions of Christianity in America are still perceived by non-whites as largely the "property" of whites. These racial disparities, moreover, perpetuate the alienation of millions of Christians of Color in the United States.

---

17   "David Masci, "Europe projected to retain its Christian majority, but religious minorities will grow," Pew Research Center, April 15, 2015, accessed September 8, 2016, http://www.pewresearch.org/fact-tank/2015/04/15/europe-projected-to-retain-its-christian-majority-but-religious-minorities-will-grow/; Robert P. Jones, "The Eclipse of White Christian America," The Atlantic, July 12, 2016, accessed September 8, 2016, http://www.theatlantic.com/politics/archive/2016/07/the-eclipse-of-white-christian-america/490724/.

18   Philip Jenkins, The Next Christendom: The Coming of Global Christianity (Oxford: Oxford University Press, 2011); Robert P. Jones, "The Eclipse of White Christian America"; "The Shifting Religious Identity of Latinos in the United States," Pew Research Center, May 7, 2014, accessed September 8, 2016, http://www.pewforum.org/2014/05/07/the-shifting-religious-identity-of-latinos-in-the-united-states/; "A Religious Portrait of African-Americans," Pew Research Center, January 30, 2009, accessed September 8, 2016, http://www.pewforum.org/2009/01/30/a-religious-portrait-of-african-americans/; "Asian Americans: A Mosaic of Faiths," Pew Research Center, July 19, 2012, accessed September 8, 2016, http://www.pewforum.org/2012/07/19/asian-americans-a-mosaic-of-faiths-overview/.

19   For a recent discussion of the lack of leadership diversity among Christian institutions, see: Leroy Barber, Red, Brown, Yellow, Black, White—Who's More Precious In God's Sight?: A call for diversity in Christian missions and ministry (Jericho Books, 2014); Steve Rabey, "White male leadership persists at evangelical ministries," Religious News Service, September 6, 2016, accessed September 8, 2016, http://religionnews.com/2016/09/06/white-male-leadership-persists-at-evangelical-ministries/.

To foster racial reconciliation, structural reform, and constructive dialogue, I argue for the development of a formal project of Critical Race Theory in Christianity. What follows are my initial ruminations as to what might comprise its basic tenets. No doubt I am not the first to consider such a project, and I hope that this essay will galvanize a cohort of interested scholars to think through these ideas together in formal collaboration.

1. Community Cultural Wealth and Social Justice. From a biblical vantage point, every ethnic group of the world possesses distinct, God-given, cultural treasure/wealth. To use the language of Chicana educational theorist Tara Yosso, each culture possesses "cultural capital."[20] The inherent and eternal value of the various national cultures of the world is described in Revelation 21: 22-27 (NRSV):

> 22 I saw no temple in the city, for its temple is the Lord God the Almighty and the Lamb. 23 And the city has no need of sun or moon to shine on it, for the glory of God is its light, and its lamp is the Lamb. 24 The nations will walk by its light, and the kings of the earth will bring their glory into it. 25 Its gates will never be shut by day—and there will be no night there. 26 People will bring into it the glory and the honor of the nations. 27 But nothing unclean will enter it, nor anyone who practices abomination or falsehood, but only those who are written in the Lamb's book of life.

This passage states that the "glory and honor of the nations" will be brought into the New Jerusalem for eternity. What is this "glory

---

20   Tara J. Yosso, "Whose culture has capital? A critical race theory discussion of community cultural wealth," Race Ethnicity and Education, 8:1 (2005), 69-91, DOI: 10.1080/13613320520000341006. For further reading on religion as a source of spiritual capital, specifically for undocumented college students, see: Lindsay Pérez Huber, "Challenging Racist Nativist Framing: Acknowledging the Community Cultural Wealth of Undocumented Chicana College Students to Reframe the Immigration Debate," Harvard Educational Review, Vol. 79, No. 4 (2009).

and honor" that John is speaking of? It is interesting to note that most evangelical Bible commentaries completely overlook this text. The word "glory" which is used in this passage can also be translated as "treasure" or "wealth" of the nations. Surely John is not describing literal currency or national government coffers. I believe that he is talking about the cultural treasure or wealth of the different ethnic groups of the world. This cultural treasure includes food, music, dance, literature, architecture, etc., as well as the unique cultural personalities of the world.

One important goal of CRT in Christianity is to employ multidisciplinary theological tools to highlight the God-given cultural wealth of marginalized communities, and to leverage community cultural wealth towards the promotion of social justice and minority empowerment.

2. Voice of Color Thesis. Flowing from our unique God-given cultural treasuries and our peculiar histories and experiences of oppression in the United States, we Christians of Color form distinctive parts of the Body of Christ and uniquely reflect the image of God (1 Corinthians 12: 12-14, 18-19; Romans 12: 4-5; Genesis 1: 26-28). As such, one important role we serve is as communicators of racial issues to our white sisters and brothers of the Body of Christ who are unlikely to know about racial injustice from first-hand experience. It is necessary to state this clearly because our voices have so often been dismissed. Our perspective is not better than others, yet, flowing from our experience as unique children of God, it is distinct. To reject our perspective is akin to the eye saying to the hand, "I don't need you!" or the head telling the feet, "I don't need you!" (Romans 12: 21). At the same time, Christians of Color cannot reject membership and participation in the Body of Christ. Although sometimes tempting, it is not an option. To do so would be like a foot proclaiming, "Because I am not a hand, I do not belong to the body" or an ear saying, "Because I am not an eye, I do not belong to the body "(Romans 12: 15-16). No, God has placed us each in the Body just where He wants us to be (1 Corinthians 12:18). We

belong to one another and need each other in order to "reach unity in the faith and in the knowledge of the Son of God and become mature, attaining to the whole measure of the fullness of Christ." (Romans 12: 5; 1 Corinthians 12:21; Ephesians 4:13).

3. Racism is Ordinary. Because of sinful human nature, racism is ordinary (Genesis 8:21; Psalm 14:2-3; Psalm 51:5; Romans 3:23-24). Racism and ethnocentrism is the normal state of affairs for human beings. Left to its own devices, sinful humanity, through the means of physical and institutional violence, divides the various ethnic cultures of the world into categories of privilege and exclusion. This leads to the social construction of privileged and unprivileged "races," and the inequitable distribution of God-given socio-economic, cultural, and political resources. Such discrimination violates the manifest will of God as reflected in more than 2,000 verses of Scripture (Matthew 25:31-46; Luke 4:18-19; Luke 6:20-26; Galatians 3:28-29; Acts 10:34-35; Isaiah 58:3-12; Psalm 140:12; Psalm 146:9).

4. Christianity, Whiteness, and Colonization. During the era of European global expansion, colonial regimes created the legal category of "whiteness" as a means of divvying out socio-economic and political privilege to those of European origin and excluding People of Color from access to these same privileges. From the fifteenth through twentieth centuries, Christianity became entangled with various colonial and neo-colonial projects of whiteness. Despite many biblical admonitions to the contrary, Christianity became racialized as the civil religion and religious property of whites. This destroyed the witness of global Christianity to a watching world.

5. Disentanglement and Multidisciplinary Methods. Through the implementation of multi-disciplinary theological tools, a second major goal of CRT in Christianity is to disentangle Christianity from its recent colonial heritage and guard it from neo-colonial racial projects of any form. A further goal is to highlight the historical

and contemporary efforts of those such as Bartolomé de Las Casas, Sor Juana Inés de la Cruz, Toyohiko Kagawa, Gordon Hirabayashi, César Chávez, Martin Luther King, Jr., and Alexia Salvatierra, who have resisted the historical and contemporary racist hijacking of Christianity. As a multidisciplinary project, moreover, CRT in Christianity encourages the development of multi-disciplinary theological methods involving history, law, literature, sociology, economics, and other disciplines of the humanities and social sciences.

6. The Beloved Community. The goal of Critical Race Theory in Christianity is the Beloved Community envisioned by Scripture and the biblical witness of Rev. Dr. Martin Luther King, Jr (Revelation 5:9-10, 7:9-10; Galatians 3:28-29; John 10: 16; Ephesians 2:14-21; Colossians 1:15-20; Acts 10:34-35). Done in the spirit of love and the empowerment of Jesus Christ, the ultimate goal of CRT in Christianity is the reconciliation of all people from every cultural and ethnic background. CRT in Christianity celebrates and embraces the diverse, God-given cultures of the world, but it is not ethnocentric. It seeks the shalom and reconciliation of all humanity in Jesus Christ. This unifying and hopeful eschatological vision represents a distinct contribution to the broader field of Critical Race Theory.

Conclusion

Julio was a non-traditional student in my introductory course on Chicana/o history, identity, and culture. This course provides a historical overview of Mexican American history and explores such topics as the racial caste system of colonial Mexico, Asian-Latinos, Manifest Destiny and the U.S.-Mexico War, Latino segregation, César Chávez and the farmworkers movement, educational inequality, and undocumented immigration. Like many Latina/o students, Julio was drawn to the class because he was curious about his own cultural heritage and the various social justice issues addressed in the course.

Before coming to UCLA, Julio was a gang member for many years in South L.A. and spent hard time as an inmate at Pelican Bay, one of the toughest prisons in the nation. After his time of incarceration and rehabilitation, Julio attended East Los Angeles Community College and eventually transferred to UCLA. As a non-traditional student, he struggled both academically and financially. On New Year's Eve, two weeks after the completion of my class, Julio searched for my email address online to tell me the bad news that he was going to quit school. Things had become too hard. As he was doing his Google search, he stumbled across Jesus for Revolutionaries. Since it was free, he downloaded it onto his computer and spent the next six hours reading and engaging with it. In the early hours of New Year's Day, Julio committed his life to God, and, through the spiritual fortitude he received from Jesus, he decided to continue his education at UCLA.

Julio's story reflects the non-traditional educational trajectory and urban life experience of thousands—perhaps millions-- of Students of Color throughout the nation. They pursue their university education not just to make money and pursue the "American Dream," but because they want to understand the structural inequalities which shape their communities and seek a profession which will equip them to bring about transformational change. Just as importantly, they desire a religious faith which will empower them to become agents of justice and social renewal. In the words of another student, "I don't want to just do social justice activities on my own all the time. I have this void in my heart when I do that. I want to know that God is with me and that I'm fulfilling God's calling and vocation."

As this essay has attempted to show, Students of Color like Julio live their lives in a spiritual borderlands. In their Ethnic Studies courses they gain vital knowledge about social injustice and structural inequality, but they are also often disparaged about the Christian faith of their grandparents, mothers, fathers, and community. On the other hand, in most Christian spaces, they face tremendous pressure to conform to a white, middle class, American imaginary of faith, history, politics, and society. This is too much for many to handle, and, like Paul and Rosa of our earlier vignettes, this quandary jettisons them into a downward emotional and spiritual spiral.

Drawing from my own experience in the Christian-Ethnic Studies borderlands, one goal of this essay is to promote discussion about the role of religion within my own academic disciplines of Chicana/o Studies, Asian American Studies, and Ethnic Studies. I hope to nurture more religious toleration in our classes, curriculum, research agendas, and professional spaces. A myriad of viewpoints about religion is crucial to the academic mission of the university. We need to have critical conversations about the negative, indeed devastating, impact which the institutions of Christianity have had upon our Communities of Color. That is vitally important. At the same time, however, it is impossible to understand the experience of our Communities of Color without also considering the positive role which religion has played, and continues to play, in our families, communities, and movements of social justice. I believe we do our students a disservice if we do the former, but neglect the latter. Furthermore, the unbalanced disparagement of the spiritual lineage of our families and communities creates an intolerable hostile campus climate and stifles academic freedom of expression.

A second goal of this essay is to raise critical consciousness among Christian churches and institutions of higher education. Please stop trying to make us white. I know this is not what you are trying to do, but this is what you are doing nonetheless. Please take off your "color-blind" lens and see things from the perspective of millions of Christians of Color in the United States. We are your sisters and brothers. Our deep concerns for structural change in education, politics, housing, healthcare, policing, mass incarceration, and voting are not going to go away because a white politician or conservative political movement forms a fragile alliance with the evangelical Christian community, or cries, even louder, that racism does not exist. Racial inequality is our reality. God is our God, too, and we know that Jesus has seen our affliction and given heed to our cry. God is aware of our sufferings and is coming to deliver us (Exodus 3:7-8; Luke 4:18-19).

Lastly, I have proposed Critical Race Theory in Christianity as one framework to help advance a larger discussion of Race and the Church. Christianity has been abused historically as a powerful earthly institution of racial oppression, but it has also inspired countless social justice movements as a source of spiritual capital for the liberation of oppressed peoples.

It is my prayer that CRT in Christianity can facilitate the disentanglement of Christianity with its colonial legacy and advance the biblical vision of racial reconciliation and liberatory praxis.

Dr. Jeney Park-Hearn

 teaches in the area of pastoral care and practical theology at Seattle University. She is an active member at Blaine Memorial United Methodist Church.

Prayers of Lament:
Making Space for Our Disenfranchised Grief

By Jeney Park-Hearn

Sitting with a pastoral counselor, I described to her the feeling of standing on the edge of a precipice, peering over a cliff, and facing the enormity of a bottomless pit that could engulf me. This was my response to a question posed about my experience with sadness. With that moment my curiosity about sadness ignited and it was kismet that it became a central feature of my doctoral studies project. Why did I experience sadness this way? What was I sad about? Was this a "normal" experience? Through qualitative research and the study of pastoral care literature about grief, I have learned that the socioreligious context of the United States informs an ethnic experience that obfuscates the reasons for many second generation Korean American Christians to grieve and to take seriously the losses that dot the interior landscape of our being Asian in the U.S.

Growing up in a Korean American family in the 1970s and 1980s I immediately began to consider the implications of emigration and immigration and the all too familiar narratives about hybrid (of course, this was not a term we used to describe ourselves during the 80s) identity and the sacrifices our parents made to transplant themselves to a strange land for the sake of their children's future. And so our families became American, insofar as the pursuit of the American Dream made it reasonable and justifiable to relinquish family ties, to traverse thousands of miles, and to leave homeland with only a few dollars to their name. This storyline, accurate or not, became an important feature of what it means to be Asian American and despite the questions that have been raised about the demands placed on immigrant families to survive by pushing individuals and families to breaking points, this story is ours. Given the hardships endured in this new "homeland," my parents' and our family's experience in the United States seemed a reasonable starting place to sort through and analyze the sadness I described to my pastoral counselor.

In the case of the Korean American immigrant community, it would be shortsighted to overlook other factors, beyond the classic American Dream storyline, that informed decisions to leave. To put another way, how did our Korean American parents experience their homeland such that a future there was not one to be embraced and hoped for? What was their Korea? Questions like this extend our gaze to Korea's historical context that shaped the Korea our parents left in wave upon wave. To disregard the ineradicable and costly ways the Korean War devastated the country and its people and necessitated emigration to the United States would be shortsighted and ill advised. In fact there is the belief that had the war not been fought, emigration to the States would not have been at the levels it has been since the signing of the Armistice in 1953.

Many first generation Korean Americans, particularly those who were part of the largest wave of immigrants from South Korea[1] were school-aged during the active years of the war and during the post war years when the country scrambled to resurrect itself from the devastation of the war as a newly defined nation,[2] cut-off by the division of the north from the south and the resultant separation from half of its land and people. The agonizing experience of family separations, fear, loss, poverty, and hunger are preserved in the memories and stories articulated by this generation of immigrants. Needless to say, the Korean War was traumatic for the people of Korea. Trauma literature abounds with study, field research, and personal memoirs that examine how the effects of traumatic events are transmitted from first generation trauma survivors to subsequent generations. The literature demonstrates that in implicit and explicit ways, subsequent generations are affected. My project explores the grief experience of second

---

1   Pyong Gap Min, Koreans' Immigration to the U.S.: History and Contemporary Trends. (New York: The Research Center for Korean Community, 2011), 7. By 1968, the Immigration Act of 1965 was in effect. The Act abolished racist immigration laws biased in favor of immigrants from northwestern European countries. More than 95% of Korean American immigrants and their children arrived after the enactment of this law.

2   Min, Koreans' Immigration, 8, 9. In 1970 the per capita income in South Korea was $251 and during the 1970s and 1980s the prospects for employment were low, as was the standard of living.

generation Korean American Christians (SGKAC) related to the Korean War and to immigration and also engages pastoral care literature in order to build a pastoral response to the particularity of their grief. Given the predominance of intrapersonal approaches to understanding grief and human responses to it,[3] it is tempting to expect that proper grieving entails that the generation that directly experienced the war and subsequent generations must be fully conscious of the Korean War and all related losses so as to fully emote and thereby go through the necessary processes related to loss. While there is value in being aware and conscious, this project argues that the lived experience of grief for second generation Korean American Christians does not necessarily fit the normative grief process that is widely accepted and standardized in pastoral care literature because their loss and grief are not fully acknowledged. Korean Americans are racialized subjects whose constructed identities impede the conscious recognition of the legacy of loss.

Through family narratives about the Korean War, emigration, and immigration my project contends that loss and grief have not been fully recognized and processed by SGKAC. It will call for a more blurred boundary between suffering and celebration and will problematize theologies of victory that do not allow for the reality of broken relationships, unacknowledged grief, the absence of mourning, and unprocessed loss.

Through the concept of disenfranchised grief, my interdisciplinary project asserts that SGKACs' unawareness of their loss and grief is impeded by societal, cultural, and historical factors. Rather than address this from a psychodynamic approach that privileges the intrapsychic dynamics of interior life and holds the individual accountable for unawareness, my project is constructionist in approach and scrutinizes some of the sociocultural and historical factors that have informed and shaped Asian American identity through narratives. The research participants in this study demonstrate that they are able to maintain relationships, contribute to their communities, and live productive lives despite the milieu of loss that sur-

---

3   Elizabeth Kubler-Ross made widely popular the theory that individuals experience grief as comprised by denial, anger, bargaining, depression, and acceptance. See Elisabeth Kubler-Ross, On Death and Dying: What the Dying Have to Teach Doctors, Nurses, Clergy, and Their Own Families (New York: Scribner, 1969).

rounds their lives. Their lives problematize literature and scholarship that defines healthy ways of processing grief and challenge pastoral caregivers to find alternative responses and to hold different expectations of individuals and communities whose grief may not be readily accessible. Rather than impose a normative experience of loss and grief, pastoral theologians must take note of disenfranchised grief and recommend helpful and validating praxis lest they further disenfranchise Korean Americans. At the same time, however, the blatant and veiled grief in the stories of research participants provide a rationale for creating hospitable and sustained spaces where grief can be recognized and held as a pathway for deepening encounters with the Sacred.

Prayers of lament, understood as the biblical tradition wherein anger, grief, despair, and protest are expressed to God,[4] is a process that can contribute to restoration and healing for SGKAC, many who are all too familiar with family discord, an intense sense of disconnection from first generation parents, and other adjustment issues shared by immigrant communities. I identify the second generation Korean American church to be a primary locus where SGKAC are invited to process their grief in community and through engaging in prayers of lament.

The Korean War

Because this project is primarily interested in appropriate pastoral responses to second generation Korean Americans and the forms of knowledge they have about the Korean War, this project will mainly draw from scholarship that will more directly inform how lamentation is a pastoral and theologically sound response to and for people affected by the Korean War. This project, while acknowledging the import of the geopolitical intricacies of the Korean War, will not produce a meta-level analysis of this ongoing conflict. Rather, this paper will address and lament the human costs of warring. From fiction to memoirs to qualitative research projects, non-Koreans and the Korean American community in diaspora

---

4   Kathleen D. Billman and Daniel L. Migliore, Rachel's Cry: Prayer of Lament and Rebirth of Hope (Cleveland: United Church Press, 1999), 6.

have revisited personal accounts of the war and as a result have not only reclaimed myriad voices that have been lost in the "Forgotten War"[5] but also humanized the face of a war that has long been overshadowed by an unsophisticated bifurcation of ideological positioning. Korean American novelists like Susan Choi and Chang Rae Lee develop characters, scripts, and plots to reanimate the devastated lives of individuals, families, and communities caught in the forced migrations from the North to the South and then further south to Pusan. Memoirist Helie Lee, in Still Life with Rice, recounts the story of her grandmother and the hardships she survived in her move from the North to the South and in the sequel to it, In the Absence of Sun, Lee chronicles the painstaking and dangerous process she and her family endured in order to reunite her grandmother with her son and his family in North Korea.[6] James A. Foley and Choong Soon Kim, through interviews and participant observation, grapple with the heart-wrenching consequences for families separated by the war. Their research also illumines the pathos of Korean families in the documentation of limited and short-lived reunions between separated family members, many who have lived for decades without knowing if loved ones have survived.[7] Psychologist Ramsey Liem and Asian American Studies scholar Grace Yoo interview Koreans and Korean North Americans to hear first hand accounts of the Korean War. Liem, motivated to dismantle the wall

---

5   Bruce Cumings writes that his earliest knowledge of the reference, the Forgotten War, to the Korean War was in a U.S. News & World Report article published in May 1951. Cumings argues that the Korean War does not register in U.S. memory as compared to World War I, World War II, and the Vietnam War because of the public perception that the U.S. was not affected by the Korean War. As such, veterans of the Korean War feel ignored and forgotten. For the U.S. populace, the Korean War is "just another transient episode among a myriad of interventions in Third World countries that do not bear close examination." Bruce Cumings, The Korean War: A History (New York: Modern Library, 2010), 62, 63.

6   See Susan Choi, The Foreign Student (New York: Harper Collins, 1998); Chang Rae Lee, The Surrendered: A Novel (New York: Penguin Books, 2010); Helie Lee, Still Life with Rice: A Young American Woman Discovers the Life and Legacy of Her Korean Grandmother (New York: Touchstone, 1996); Helie Lee, In the Absence of the Sun: A Korean American Woman's Promise to Reunite Three Lost Generations of Her Family (New York: Harmony Books, 2002).

7   See Foley, Korea's Divided Families and Choong Soon Kim, Faithful Endurance: An Ethnography of Korean Family Dispersal (Tucson: University of Arizona Press, 1988).

of silence that surrounds the war, interviews thirty-six Korean American men and women to hear them describe their lived experience of the war.[8] Researching and writing from a feminist hermeneutic, Yoo's interest is in the lives of Korean American women who were mothers during the war.[9] The scholarship of Liem and Yoo are exceptional in that scant attention has been given to Korean Americans and the meanings they attribute to their experience of the Korean War.[10][11]

These and other works reveal the spectrum of human response to the devastation of war that all too often can be lost amidst figures that account for casualties and that quantify war-related loss. Numbers are not without value, however, and for the sake of remembrance, I include here statistics depicting the different types of casualties of the war.

Liem, who has heralded the necessity of penetrating the silence that surrounds the Korean War, provides figures that impart a picture of the vastness of the casualties incurred during the war. These include 3 million civilians (10 % of the population), 10 million separated from families, a destroyed physical and social infrastructure, half a million North Korean soldiers, 175,000 South Korean soldiers, 500,000 Chinese volunteers, 37,000 U.S. soldiers, and 3,000 UN forces.[12]

The magnitude of loss and the ripple effect of these numbers, the emotional scars of displacement, the debilitating effects of physical illness, the impending death for the physically ill, the anguish of not knowing the

---

8   See Ramsay Liem, "Silencing Historical Trauma: The Politics and Psychology of Memory and Voice," Peace and Conflict: Journal of Peace Psychology 13, no. 2 (2007); Liem, "War and the Art of Remembering: Korean Americans and the 'Forgotten War,'" The International Journal of Interdisciplinary Social Sciences 3, no. 7, (2008); Grace Yoo, "A Not So Forgotten War," Peace Review 16, no. 2 (2004).

9   Yoo, "A Not So Forgotten War," 170.

10   Liem observes this dearth of research and scholarship on Korean Americans' experience of the war. Ramsay Liem, "Silencing Historical Trauma: The Politics and Psychology of Memory and Voice," Peace and Conflict: Journal of Peace Psychology

11   , no. 2 (2007): 154. Liem directs a multimedia exhibit of the Korean War, Still Present Pasts: Korean Americans and the "Forgotten War," in an effort to visually and orally give public expression to unspoken private memories and narratives. Liem, "War and the Art of Remembering: Korean Americans and the 'Forgotten War,'" International Journal of Interdisciplinary Social Sciences 3, no. 7, (2008): 111.

12   Liem, "Silencing," 154.

welfare of loved ones, and the countless challenges for any national infra-structure to rebuild a nation that has been crushed is more than daunting. The horrors of the Korean War are concretized in the numbers and above statistics that represent human lives.

Emigration and Immigration

The impassioned pleas of individuals and communities and the intrac-table deadlocks that characterize today's current debate concerning im-migration policy in the United States belie the fact that people had set foot on this land centuries before the arrival of its European immigrant settlers. The arbitrary nature of centuries-long international politics and power plays that construct notions of citizenship and national boundaries are long forgotten.

All countries are affected by a global web that connects humanity. And motivations for leaving homeland are evidence of the havoc that ensues when nations and alliances vie for limited resources, military dominance, and political rule, to name a few. While the aim of this project is not to attend to Korea's vast and long history, it is important to remember and acknowledge the debilitating decades of Japanese occupation that ren-dered Korea exposed and vulnerable to outside and competing interests and culminating in the Korean War and post-war years. Korean emigra-tion to the United States has been conceptualized through the language and imagery of waves.[13] The third wave (1965-1990) is the most relevant to my project in that all of the parents of the research participants emi-grated during this time. Economic uncertainty and the oppressive nature of military rule were factors that pushed Koreans to seek a better life in

---

13   Following the first wave of Korean Christian immigrants, who arrived in significant numbers to work on the sugar plantations in Hawaii in the early 1900s, the second wave (1950-1964) was predominantly comprised of women who married United States service-men and who emigrated to join their husbands. The U.S. military presence in Korea is also linked to the large number of Amerasian orphans who were born to Korean women and servicemen.   Many of these infants and children were adopted and brought to the U.S. during this second wave. It is also during these years and it is estimated that up to 6,000 Korean students, in pursuit of higher education, emigrated to the U.S. See Pyong Gap Min, Koreans' Immigration, 2-6.

the U.S. Additionally, the threat of another catastrophic war loomed large in the psyches of the Korean people. While these push factors[14] can be explicitly linked to the devastating effects of the Korean War, sociologist and Korean American studies scholar Pyong Gap Min extends the discussion about immigration by examining Korea's ties with the U.S. and how these have formed an intricately bound matrix of economic, political, and military dependency that make possible the inroads to the United States. He argues that the Korean wives of United States servicemen of the second immigration wave made possible, through the sponsorship of kin, the entry of thousands of Koreans. Grace Yoo writes about this quieted immigration phenomenon and the shame that surrounds the Korean sex industry related to the United States military and the thousands of Korean sisters, aunts, daughters, nieces, and mothers whose pasts remain a secret. The subsequent generations of Korean Americans stand on the shoulders, bodies of these women.[15] Korean immigration is so intricately tied to the Korean War that Chang Minyong, who was interviewed by Liem makes the statement that if it weren't for the Korean War; he would not be in the United States.[16] Similarly, the impact of the Korean War on emigration is made plain in the title of Ji-Yeon Yuh's journal article, "Moved by War: Migration, Diaspora, and the Korean War."

While it is obvious that first generation immigrant parents faced myriad challenges and hardships, these are somehow rendered invisible by portrayals of Korean American families who "make it" and who send their children to prestigious Ivy League colleges. These "success" stories justify the toil and labor, the discrimination, and other vicissitudes that characterize life in a society where racism and xenophobia are not vestiges but

---

14   The push-pull theory was developed to explain immigration dynamics and the forces that cause migration. Push factors are the circumstances in the country of origin that compel individuals and families to emigrate. These can include economic hardship, political instability, and environmental difficulties. Pull factors make the destination country appealing because of the perceived opportunities for an improved life. Philip Q. Yang, "A Theory of Asian Immigration to the United States," Journal of Asian American Studies 13, no. 1 (2010): 2, doi: 10.1353/jaas.0.0061.

15   Grace M. Cho, Haunting the Korean Diaspora: Shame Secrecy, and the Forgotten War (Minneapolis: University of Minnesota Press, 2008), 1-4.

16   Ramsay Liem, "History Trauma, and Identity: The Legacy of the Korean War for Korean Americans," Amerasia Journal 29, no. 3 (2003-2004): 118.

rather the norm. As American mainstream culture continues to recognize and to applaud the achievements of "Whiz Kid"[17] Asian Americans, the narratives of those who are mired in the daily struggle to survive are and will be silenced by comparisons to those who have "made it." Immigration deals tough blows to individuals, families, and communities, causing great harm to psyches, systems, and affiliations. Mental health is compromised as family systems buckle under the weight of survival and broken relationships, and communities are overwhelmed in their efforts to be exemplary citizens even with the gnawing sense that something is wrong. The second generation Korean American church must not be distracted by the quest to adhere to triumphalist doctrines and tenets, at the cost of being unresponsive to the suffering people in our communities. The vicissitudes of immigration do not result solely from that which transpires when people arrive in the States from destinations around the world. Oftentimes, circumstances in their home country lead people to make poignant decisions to emigrate. Present day images of South Korea's prosperity and advancement tempt the world to forget the already Forgotten War[18] and its indelible imprint on the lives of thousands upon thousands of people who directly experienced its horrors, many who are now Korean American immigrants. The lives of their children and the family conflicts that have become so familiar to the Korean American community bear witness to the effects of this war through the stories, silences, emotions, beliefs, and mood states brought to the parent-child dynamic via our emigrated parent(s) who experienced the war, the immense poverty that resulted, and in the division of the country that left thousands of families separated from family members in the north or south. Somehow these embedded losses register in the souls and psyches of individuals, families, and communities in such a way that sadness could be an expected affective response. In many ways, however, these losses do not register as losses to be mourned and, while the success stories of many first and second generation Korean Ameri-

---

17   David Brand authored an article referring to Asian American youth as whiz kids because of their academic success and their entry into elite colleges and universities. See David Brand, "The New Whiz Kids," Time Magazine, August 1987.

18   Ramsay Liem, "'So I've Gone Around in Circles…' Living the Korean War," Amerasia Journal 31, no. 3 (2005): 157.

cans leave the superficial impression that all is well, a pastoral response is necessary.

The seductive power of the success story infiltrates the Korean American church and its images of faithful living. Even in the realm of religious life and faith, the "Whiz Kid"[19] nomenclature persists as "successful" evangelical Korean American young adults receive ecclesial and scholarly attention and accolades. These subtle and normalized depictions of Korean Americans' success lure many Korean American churches into triumphalist attitudes that leave little room for stories that present counter-narratives of mental illness, poverty, addiction, divorce, suicide, and other tales of "failure." And so, Korean American churches readily espouse theologies of triumph and victory that are consistent with the templates of Asian American success that permeate the American landscape. Even as Korean American churches recognize the reality of suffering in the Passion of Christ, it is for a moment that we hover, not land, in this hard place, where there is a distinct border readily and eagerly crossed over to join in the celebration of Christ's resurrection. Theologies of victory and triumphalism are in danger of further disenfranchising the loss and grief of SGKAC. To be responsive to suffering is to bear witness to the innumerable and diverse expressions of pain and struggle shared by humanity, thus situating the witnessing church in a receptive position to encounter God who suffers.[20] If God is incarnational, then church life and theology must reflect the everyday, mundane, imperfect quality of lived experience. This is the space between Good Friday and Easter Sunday.

---

19   Rebecca Y. Kim utilizes this terminology in reference to Asian American evangelicals who attend elite colleges and universities in the United States and comprise more than half the membership of evangelical Christian groups on these campuses. See Rebecca Y. Kim, God's New Whiz Kids?: Korean American Evangelicals on Campus (New York: New York University Press, 2006).

20   Douglas John Hall argues that God, who takes human suffering seriously, must suffer and does suffer in order to be God with us. Douglas John Hall, God and Human Suffering: An Exercise in the Theology of the Cross (Minneapolis: Augsburg Publishing House, 1986), 34, 35.

Research Project

In my qualitative research project I conducted semi-structured inter-views with nine second generation Korean American young adult Christians (four men and five women) in their thirties and early forties and asked the same series of open-ended questions to each research participant. The socioeconomic status and the level of educational attainment varied amongst the respondents.

Needless to say, each interview experience was different despite the fact that I asked the same series of questions about their recollections of stories about the Korean War and about their parents' immigration to the U.S. Each research participant varied in the amount of detail they provided about their parents' lives during the years leading up to the Korean War. Some shared general information about family members escaping to the south while others outlined a chronology of events of the move from present day North Korea to points south. Generally, most research participants had impressions and vague ideas about how their parents survived during Korea's post-war years. Stories recounting the early years in the U.S. were more detailed with memories of hardship, blue-collar jobs, and sacrifice. Handling the particularities of each family and respecting the unique circumstances faced by each, I was able to recognize similar challenges and patterns of events that featured in the diversity of experience. Broadly speaking, the research participants who shared stories of post-war Korea associated it with poverty, hunger, lack of opportunity, the U.S. military, or-phans, and death. On the one hand, the interview data showed consistently an image of the U.S. as savior and hero to South Korea, the land of opportunity, morally superior to Korea, and as a new home. On the other, a few research participants were also critical of ongoing U.S. presence in South Korea and questioned popularly held perceptions of the Korean War that depict the U.S. rescuing South Korea.

The accounts of family stories about the Korean War and the early immigration years reveal loss on numerous levels. According to Kenneth R. Mitchell and Herbert Anderson, loss is experienced in personal, relational, and societal realms and includes intrapsychic, material, role, functional, relationship, and systemic losses. In light of the myriad types of loss, the analysis of the interview material revealed five themes were more apparent than others: the legacy of the Korean War, losses related to the Korean War and immigration, distance from loss, identity conflict, and dominant narratives of the United States.

Research Findings and Prevailing Narratives

The social context of the U.S. and the myths and narratives that play a prominent role in the shaping of human experience are inclusive of people groups, so long as it is possible to lump people together according to any defining feature, visible or not. Given that racial microaggressions and microinvalidations[21] can construct the perception of reality for Asian Americans and also lead to a "healthy paranoia" about the dominant culture,[22] I am fully cognizant of the perspective that shapes my interpretation of the research data as well as the cultural and sociopolitical milieu in which the research participants' stories reside. This is important because the history depicts the marginalizing cultural context that gives rise to seminal efforts to privilege the subjective experience of Asian Americans.

As the researcher for this project, I have a significant role in shaping a story that emerges from the stories shared by the research participants. Each interview depicts the uniqueness of each research participant's experience and narrative analysis seeks to understand, for one, how and why a story has been told in a particular way. The aim is not to discover a fact that is generalizable to an entire population but rather to disclose "conceptual inferences about a social process."[23] By interrogating the interview data with a dialogic/performance analytical method operating,[24] I studied

---

21 Derald Wing Sue, Microaggressions in Everyday Life: Race, Gender, and Sexual Orientation (Hoboken, NJ: John Wiley and Sons, 2010), 5, 25, 29, 37.

22 Derald Wing Sue, Microaggressions, 73.

23 Catherine Kohler Riessman, Narrative Analysis (Newbury Park, CA: Sage Publications, 1993), 13.

24 This method, in its engaging the telling dimension of a narrative, operates out of the view that narratives are co-constructed and that the back and forth of human talk builds a dialogue that is a performed narrative. Constructionist in orientation, this method understands that stories are not formed in a vacuum, far removed from the influencing power of

the interviews with a hermeneutics of suspicion resulting from a cultural context of racial microaggressions that also contribute to a particular shaping of a meta-narrative of the interviews. A hermeneutics of suspicion privilege the perspective that stereotypes and myths as narratives (U.S. as asylum, the American Dream, Yellow Peril, perpetual foreigner, model minority myth) marginalize and have a constraining and normalizing effect on Asian Americans. In other words, these narratives establish artificial structures of personality and identity that can define normative ways of being Asian American. Consider the media portrayals of the type-casted Asian person and family, the personas they embody, and their place in a broader social context. Stereotypes and national narratives are powerful because they are doggedly persistent and readily available to individual and social consciousness. The double bind of the model minority myth and perpetual foreigner status results in a tenuous position for Asians in the U.S. and warrants an ever-cautious posture regarding how Asians are perceived. In order to explicate more fully the political contexts out of which narratives emerge, any attempt to interpret stories must include "writing out the social."[25] To omit this crucial step protects prevailing dominant discourses and foreclose the possibility of different interpretations of any given narrative.[26]

Second generation Korean American Christians have experienced loss. These losses are related to a war that was not experienced directly and to the struggles of immigration that are all too familiar. While research participants did not directly experience the Korean War, their oftentimes-piecemeal knowledge of the War provides a picture of the dire circumstances their parents knew. Echoing the message of the American Dream

---

cultures, society, and history, to name a few. Rather, narratives are embedded in a myriad of shaping forces whose implications must be acknowledged and probed. "Stories are social artifacts, telling us as much about society and culture as they do about a person or group. How do these contexts enter into storytelling? How is a story co-produced in a complex choreography—in spaces between teller and listener, speaker and setting, text and reader, and history and culture?" Reissman, Narrative Methods, 105, 107.

25 Catrina Brown and Tod Augusta-Scott, "Introduction: Postmodernism, Reflexivity, and Narrative Therapy," in Narrative Therapy: Making Meaning, Making Lives, ed. Catrina Brown and Tod Augusta-Scott (Thousand Oaks, CA: Sage Publications, 2007), x.

26 Brown and Augusta-Scott, "Introduction," xi.

and the invitation to find refuge in the U.S., research participants know that their parents suffered and that their prospects for a good life in post-War Korea were bleak, pushing them to leave their homeland for a better life in the U.S. Research participants admit that they do not know enough about the War while having the expectation of themselves that they should know more about their Korean roots. They live with a longing and curiosity about the land of their people and do not find it odd to root for Korea or to have the desire to align with Korean students who participate in anti-U.S. protests. Research participants know that migration required of their parents courage, strength, and risk and that their parents had the foresight to migrate for the welfare and benefit of the second generation. Knowing this, they are grateful and hold a deep respect and admiration for their parents.

Established in the U.S., the research participants talk about their extended family members in Korea and their encounters with familiar strangers to whom they are closely related yet far removed in context, language, habits, and lifestyle. And while most research participants did not explicitly use the words loss and grief, I frame the significance of these ambivalent ties as loss, based on pastoral theological scholarship that includes the loss of relationships in the category of loss. The multiple and tragic losses of the Korean War that first generation Korean Americans experienced live on in SGKAC. Research participants presume the enduring effects of the Korean War on the first generation, and so in their attempts to understand parental idiosyncrasies, they factor in the War.

The personal struggles with identity and the questions about ethnic and racial identification feed the relentless doubts about belonging in a context where the white American experience is normalized and yearned for, even as research participants slip in and out of Korean and American worlds and the expectations and encumbrances therein. As such, research participants are haunted by the vastness of what is unknown about Korea and the expectation that they should know more.

Situated in between their Korean and American contexts, where a sense of belonging is ephemeral and fleeting, SGKAC manage to negotiate who they are and to fit in where they can. Except for their references to the American Dream narrative, the research participants did not explicitly name or discuss the stereotypes and myths that have narrated the Asian American experience.

As the researcher and the co-constructor of a meta-story that emerges from the interviews, I discuss the themes that surface from their stories through the lens informed by the myths and persistent narratives that racialize Asian Americans subjectivity. I cast these as what I call disenfranchising instruments and acknowledge that I extrapolate certain meanings from their stories. I also give full consideration of the view that we do not arrive at knowledge in a vacuum but through all elements of context, including the interpretive moves of the researcher.

My questions prompted their recollection of family stories and I learned that the Korean War is usually not a topic of their personal and conscious reflections. All nine research participants recalled stories shared by various family members and one research participant also indicated that she had researched the Korean War on her own for answers to her questions about it. An obvious way that second generation Korean Americans have been affected by the Korean War is through the immigration that ensued on account of the hardships of post-war Korea. Parents of research participants talk about the opportunity to better one's life in the U.S. and while this cannot be isolated as the sole reason for emigration, this link implicates the Korean War and its role in catalyzing mass movement out of Korea.

Some of the stories suggest a pervasive quality of the Korean War and how its influence extended into the immigration years and into the lives of SGKAC through the parenting they experienced and the palpable hardships of their parents' lives they witnessed. Needless to say, the hardships faced by first generation immigrants are duly noted and helpful to the work of mitigating their marginalized experience. In the same vein, research involving the progeny of first generation immigrants illumine their unique experience of immigration and inform efforts to respond to the challenges they encounter.[27]

The model minority myth, the successful immigrant narrative, the American Dream narrative, and the portrayal of Asian Americans as per-

---

27   For an example of such a study see Min Zhou, "Growing Up American: The Challenge Confronting Immigrant Children and Children of Immigrants," Annual Review of Sociology 23 (1997), accessed September 30, 2013, JSTOR.

petual foreigners convey conflicting messages that at best result in racial identity ambivalence. The effect of these dominant narratives is to consign Asian Americans to a script that showcases success, talent, giftedness, and hard work, all based on a system of meritocracy. The dominance of the interminable notion of the American Dream and the widely held view that Asian Americans have achieved this renders questionable, and isolates to the fringes, experiences of loss and pain that have the capacity to undermine the widely held notion that the normative Asian American is privileged, not a foreigner, and is accepted into mainstream America. Given the U.S. context where Asian Americans are establishing home and identity and the narratives therein that obstruct access to loss and pain, the research participants demonstrate their knowledge of loss related to the Korean War and immigration. The interviews also reveal a sense of detachment from the Korean War and confusion about identity. This ambivalence coupled with the disenfranchising effects of dominant narratives dilutes the experience and expression of loss.[28]

Grief

Secular and faith-based practitioners and scholars in the numerous helping professions would not hesitate to dispense advice and counsel to those who have experienced loss that grieving is necessary for well-being. In fact, their wisdom is soundly informed by vast research in various disciplines in the social sciences that have over the years outlined the dynamics of loss and appropriate responses. From the widely accepted psychoanalytic view that loss must initiate a redirection of energy from the lost object to a new object, to the popular stages of grief, theories about loss and grief and the nuances therein continue to abound. Kenneth Mitchell and Herbert Anderson write about the pervasiveness of loss and associate it with the processes of attachment and separation inherent in the human condition. According to Mitchell and Anderson, these include material, relationship, intrapsychic, functional, role, and systemic losses and in response to loss,

---

28 Kenneth R. Mitchell and Herbert Anderson, All Our Losses, All Our Griefs: Resources for Pastoral Care (Philadelphia: Westminster Press, 1983), 54.

grief follows. "Grief is the normal but bewildering cluster of ordinary human emotions arising in response to a significant loss, intensified and complicated by the relationship to the person or the object lost."

Disenfranchised Grief

The processes and dynamics mentioned above are not necessarily readily accessible to or viewed to be a valid experience for any and all people who grieve. Kenneth Doka has introduced caregivers, mental health professionals, and thanatologists to a nuanced understanding of bereavement and its related responses and process through the concept of "disenfranchised grief." Emerging from his astute and careful clinical observations, disenfranchised grief points to an ever-expansive feature of loss wherein societal rules and mores, cultural expectations, and historical circumstances impede the capacity to recognize and validate loss in certain people. This concept also points to the processes that impede the recognition of grief in communities and the individual lives therein.

In writing about disenfranchised grief, Doka argues that amongst the psychological, biological, and sociological facets of grief, the social aspect has received the least amount of attention. Individuals and communities whose grief is disenfranchised do not have 'the right to grieve.' "That right to grieve may not be accorded for many reasons, such as the ways a person grieves, the nature of the loss, or the nature of the relationship. So, although the person experiences grief, that grief is not openly acknowledged, socially validated, or publicly observed."[29]

That this phenomenon exists is not implausible considering the social context in which feelings, thoughts, and behaviors are deemed appropriate or valid in accord with established and concretized norms and expectations. Doka contends that attending to the social aspect of grief can augment our understanding of disenfranchised grief. Societal norms govern

---

29 Kenneth Doka, "Introduction," in Disenfranchised Grief: New Directions, Challenges, and Strategies for Practice, ed. Kenneth Doka (Champaign: Research Press, 2002), 5. 29 Doka references the work of A. R. Hochschild to demonstrate the powerful shaping influence of societal rules and norms in regulating behavior, cognitions, and affect.

and shape thoughts, feelings, and behaviors through 'rules' for each dimension of human experience.[30] For example, the following two statements demonstrate the influence of these rules. "I know I should not feel guilty." "I have every right to feel angry."[31]

Similarly, thinking rules and spiritual rules also deem what is acceptable and within the parameters of reason and proper belief, respectively. Thinking rules are apparent in statements that question how a person can think a certain way. The espousal of spiritual rules is evident in the invalidation of grief evident in the assumption that grief is not necessary because the person who has died is now in a better place.

According to Doka, all societies have grieving rules that warrant the circumstances and situations that elicit grief, that identify legitimate grievers, that outline necessary and proper responses to grief, and that discerns the valid recipients of support and care. U.S. grieving rules, for instance, restrict the number of legitimate grievers when someone has died, to members of the family, when in fact the network of meaningful individuals to any given person might include non-family members. The countless ways that people encounter the loss of relationships, jobs, pets, home, and health, amongst others is met by grief responses that fall within or beyond socially sanctioned norms. Behaviors that do not "fit" into the categories of acceptable grief expression are not recognized, thereby rendering the grief disenfranchised.[32] Doka and Terry L. Martin acknowledge and challenge the bias in Western counseling culture that has construed assumptions about grief and contends that the privileging of affect has not afforded support for expressions of grief that are less emotive.[33]

Herbert Anderson, in writing about the hiddenness of men's grief, underscores the valuation of particular grief experiences that are unique to person and to context. According to Anderson, because men grieve in secret, they are isolated in their experience. In their experiences of loss, they

---

30   Doka references the work of A. R. Hochschild to demonstrate the powerful shaping influence of societal rules and norms in regulating behavior, cognitions, and affect.

31   Doka, "Introduction," 6.

32   Doka, "Introduction," 6, 7.

33   Terry L. Martin and Kenneth J. Doka, Men Don't Cry- Women Do: Transcending Gender Stereotypes of Grief (Philadelphia: Brunner/Mazel, 2000), 2, 3.

are "doubly disenfranchised" because they are not supposed to feel pain and if they do, they are certainly not supposed to express anything.[34]

In situations where men do grieve, however, the way that this is expressed is usually not recognized as grief, rendering their experience invisible to outside observers. Anderson maintains that the restrictive nature of cultural stereotypes that impede affective expressions can only be resisted by multiple attempts to grieve differently. Men assume a hyper-masculine posture that communicates strength, composure, and invincibility when they experience loss. Second, an insistence on autonomy as a strategy prevents the possibility of being hurt and maintains the image of responsibility and strength. Third, men avoid feeling vulnerable by attributing fault and weakness in others. Disdaining and ridiculing behavior defend against personal feelings of weakness. Fourth, rather than forging connection with others during times of need, men take on "fix-it mode" and assume the role of caregiver in order to feel connected without the entanglements of emotional involvement. And fifth, men present themselves as intellectual and abstract as a means of being respected and valued, and not through connection.

Cultural myths undergird these strategies and by challenging them, men will be better able to grieve. Anderson argues that the mistaken notion that men should not be vulnerable directly affects how men respond to loss.[35] Myths and stereotypes shape men's grief experience and to loosen the grip of these, Anderson identifies the inability to accept human finitude, vulnerability, and interdependence as psychological and theological barriers obstructing men's grief experiences.

Similar to the experience of men, the power and influence of myths and stereotypes have informed SGKAC's identity and what we are to expect of ourselves, including our experience with grief. The grief of SGKAC, like the research participants, is disenfranchised. The research participants were born in the U.S. and so it might not be readily comprehended that U.S. citizens experience loss with regard to Korea, and thus this relationship is not recognized.

---

34   Herbert Anderson, "Men and Grief: The Hidden Sea of Tears Without Outlet," in The Care of Men, ed. Christie Cozad Neuger and James Newton Poling (Nashville: Abingdon Press, 1997), 205.

35   Anderson, 208-10.

The model minority stereotype is implicated in the disenfranchising contexts of losses that are unacknowledged at the exclusion of grievers. As model minorities, many SGKAC have achieved the coveted American Dream and there appears to be nothing substantial to grieve and simply put, grieving belies the image of success and accomplishment. This expectation precludes SGKAC from grief because there is no room for it in the successful immigrant storyline. Also, SGKAC did not personally experience the circumstances of loss of the Korean War and so, again, there appears to be no reason to grieve. And lastly, SGKAC are not observed to be grieving, so a natural conclusion is that they must not have anything to grieve.

Prayers of Lament

Scholarship on lament abounds. Among these are biblical commentaries, pastoral care literature, discussions on ethics, and theological expositions to name a few. Scholars and advocates for the practice of lament expand upon the various ways that individuals and communities have mourned and grieved loss, injustice, death, destruction, and other forms of calamity that give wake to human suffering and anguish. Consonant throughout the wide range of research and scholarship on lament is the perspective that the practice of lament is a necessary and vital feature of lived experience.

Faced with the compelling reality of suffering and their understanding that complaint, grief, anger, and protest have a rightful place in the Christian faith and in the biblical tradition, Billman and Migliore are convinced of the import of prayers of lament and elaborate upon three experiential dimensions of these. First, they discuss these prayers as precipitated by the expected or unexpected death of a beloved family member or friend to suicide, disease, accidents, and crime. Such a loss can hurl the grieving individual into spiritual confusion and profound doubt about God's goodness and presence.[36] Second, prayers of lament are also justified for individuals and communities who are traumatized by devastating losses,

---

36   Billman and Migliore, Rachel's Cry, 8.

such as war, poverty, genocide, and homelessness. These prayers of lament and protest demand justice for undeserved suffering and seek reconciliation between perpetrators and survivors.[37] While Billman and Migliore include reconciliation as an element of prayers of lament, because reconciliation requires the articulation of the voices of those who have suffered injustice and devastation, I think it is critical to be cognizant of timing and how soon reconciliation can be authentically engaged, given the quest for justice. Third, and distinct from those whose lamenting are explicit in the face of tragic and devastating circumstances, are the silent and unnoticed grief-stricken, whose losses are not as apparent, as with disenfranchised grief, and yet profoundly felt.

Billman and Migliore discuss the absence of lament in churches and in the broader society and conclude that without lament, other aspects of Christian faith including ministry, prayer, service, and worship to name a few, would be void and lacking in robustness.[38] A church that is uncomfortable with lament and/or believes that its place in the life of the church is unwarranted, is detached from the suffering around the world, is immune to the plight of creation at the mercy of exploitative human hands.[39] Further, I argue that the church that does not lament renders its congregants disconnected to loss and to the healing made possible when people grieve together. By this I mean that an inability to lament keeps individuals and communities disconnected, unaware, and removed from pain and without the knowledge and comfort that God is in the midst of our loss. To include in the life of the church a process of lament that raises awareness and restores connection with God is solid pastoral praxis.

In the church, however, there exists ambivalence about prayers of lament, which reflects a general societal vacillation concerning negative emotions, including grief. Situated between the pressure to avoid personal and corporate pain by wearing a brave and hopeful face and the popularized therapeutic advice to feel all human emotion in their immediate presence, broadly speaking, American culture is puzzled about the experience

---

37   Ibid., 10.
38   Ibid., 42, 43.
39   Ibid., 42.

of grief and loss and about appropriate responses.[40] Cultural critics and theologians alike have observed the American proclivity to deny failure, loss, pain, vulnerability, and death and a parallel dynamic in the mainline Christian church in the absence of a political theology of the cross. Even as the American populace faces failures and powerlessness and is daily reminded of sickness, war, and violence, a counter message to have hope and to believe in the U.S. also prevails. And yet these messages to have hope and to be optimistic collapse under the weight of the reality of multiple losses, oppression, and abuse. A way to cope with and to navigate such despair is necessary but remains elusive.[41]

Billman and Migliore proffer lament prayers as a way to reclaim a more whole expression of Christian life and prayer. The authors do not advocate a recovery of lament prayers because Christian life is supposed to be one of groans and crying. Prayers of lament are a response to the concrete reality of human struggle and when included in the broad life of faith along with prayers of thanksgiving, celebration, and joy deepen an engagement of faith amidst the wide spectrum of lived experience.[42]

Most research participants did not directly name their personal and familial sorrow in their recounting of stories related to the Korean War and to immigration. While their narratives were replete with accounts of loss, their way of talking about their experiences did not mirror the type of explicit grief expression discussed by some of the authors above. Their sharing did not exude the reality of loss they and their families have endured. As a researcher and pastoral counselor, it is of import to resist the temptation to normalize the more demonstrative and active forms of lament and thus to problematize the research participants' responses. At the same time, however, given the dynamics of disenfranchised grief and the social context in which Korean Americans reside, I cannot ignore the possibility that the research participants are in fact removed from their grief experiences that they may be minimizing such grief.

Prayers of lament as process provide a ritual and conscientizing space where SGKAC can explore their loss with the knowledge that an encoun-

---

40   Billman and Migliore, Rachel's Cry, 14, 15.

41   Ibid., 16.

42   Billman and Migliore, Rachel's Cry, 19.

ter with God awaits. Additionally and as Billman and Migliore argue, authentic hope is birthed in community when humanity wrestles with God, resists resignation, and believes God to be the source of hope. Authentic hope is grounded in reality and is not divorced from suffering. It springs forth when we have grieved and lamented loss and injustice.[43] In the articulation of protest, complaint, anger, and sadness prayers of lament resist regulating cultural representations of Asian Americans that perpetuate the expectation that compliance and docility are expected in our societal interactions but also in our ways of relating to God. In faith and trust, SGKACs can present themselves however they want, in whatever forms and know that God chooses to remain with.

Practicing Prayers of Lament

The structure and outline of biblical prayers of lament avail to the one lamenting a precise and thorough way to engage cognitions, affect, and physical responses related to personal and communal loss and unjust suffering. The wide spectrum of human anguish presumes relationship with God and the presence and steadfastness of the divine for individuals and communities who know that they suffer and who know they can express themselves before God.

Prayers of lament can be differently construed for SGKAC who can engage the features of these prayers for the purposes of validating their experience and reconfiguring and revisioning their relationship with God. Prayers of lament can function as a site of resistance wherein constraining and limiting narratives can be shed for stories that retell a person's and community's identity. Prayers of lament open up pathways and communal spaces where individuals can come together for the explicit purpose of encountering loss and grief, with the assurance that God suffers with and is most present in human struggle. The ritual acts of engaging in prayers of lament must be fortified in a church culture that understands that authentic hope can only emerge from contexts of suffering. As this message

---

43   Ibid., 124, 125.

is fortified in the life of the church, individuals will know that they do not engage their loss and grief in isolation.

Bibliography

Anderson, Herbert. "Men and Grief: The Hidden Sea of Tears Without Outlet." In The Care of Men, edited by Christie Cozad Neuger and James Newton Poling, 203-26. Nashville: Abingdon Press, 1997.

Billman, Kathleen D., and Daniel L. Migliore. Rachel's Cry: Prayer of Lament and Rebirth of Hope. Cleveland: United Church Press, 1999.

Brown, Catrina and Tod Augusta-Scott. "Introduction: Postmodernism, Reflexivity, and Narrative Therapy." In Narrative Therapy: Making Meaning, Making Lives, edited by Catrina Brown and Tod Augusta-Scott, ix-xviii. Thousand Oaks, CA: Sage Publications, 2007.

Cho, Grace M. Haunting the Korean Diaspora: Shame, Secrecy, and the Forgotten War. Minneapolis: University of Minnesota Press, 2008.

Doka, Kenneth, ed. Disenfranchised Grief: New Directions, Challenges, and Strategies for Practice. Champaign: Research Press, 2002.

Foley, James. Korea's Divided Families: Fifty Years of Separation. London: RoutledgeCurzon, 2003.

Hall, Douglas John. God and Human Suffering: An Exercise in the Theology of the Cross. Minneapolis: Augsburg Publishing House, 1986.

Kim, Choong Soon. Faithful Endurance: An Ethnography of Korean Family Dispersal. Tucson: University of Arizona Press, 1988.

Kim, Rebecca Y. God's New Whiz Kids?: Korean American Evangelicals on Campus. New York: New York University Press, 2006.

Liem, Ramsey. "Silencing Historical Trauma: The Politics and Psychology of Memory and Voice." Peace and Conflict 13, no. 2 (2007): 153-74.

--, "War and the Art of Remembering: Korean Americans and the 'Forgotten War,'" International Journal of Interdisciplinary Social Sciences 3, no. 7 (2008): 111-16.

Martin, Terry L. and Kenneth J. Doka. Men Don't Cry- Women Do: Transcending Gender Stereotypes of Grief. Philadelphia: Brunner/Mazel, 2000.

Min, Pyong Gap. "Koreans' Immigration to the U.S.: History and Contemporary Trends." New York: The Research Center for Korean Community, Queens College of CUNY, January 27, 2011.

Mitchell, Kenneth R., and Herbert Anderson. All Our Losses, All Our Griefs: Resources for Pastoral Care. Philadelphia: Westminster Press, 1983.

Riessman, Catherine Kohler. Narrative Analysis. Newbury Park, CA: Sage Publications, 1993.

Sue, Derald Wing. Microaggressions in Everyday Life: Race, Gender, and Sexual Orientation. Hoboken, NJ: John Wiley and Sons, 2010.

Yang, Philip Q. "A Theory of Asian Immigration to the United States." Journal of Asian American Studies 13, no. 1 (2010): 1-34. Accessed February 11, 2014. http://muse.jhu.edu/.

Yoo, Grace. "A Not So Forgotten War." Peace Review 16, no. 2 (2004): 169-79. Accessed February 16, 2011. Search Primer.

Zhou, Min. "Are Asian Americans Becoming White?" In Contemporary Asian America: A Multidisciplinary Reader. 2nd ed., edited by Min Zhou and James V. Gatewood, 354-59. New York: New York University Press, 2007.

↓

Narrative Articles

The Rev. Ajung Sojwal

 is an Episcopal priest, serving in the Episcopal Diocese of New York. Currently she serves as the Interim Pastor at the Church of the Divine Love, Montrose, NY.

Impact of Recent Immigrant Women Ministers in the Church

By Ajung Sojwal

Crossing cultural boundaries has been the lifeblood of historic Christianity. It is also noteworthy that most of the energy for the frontier crossing has come from the periphery rather than from the centre.

-Andrew F. Walls[1]

Our group of twelve women clergy and lay leaders took turns to introduce ourselves. Every one of us was from one Asian country or another; every one of us a first generation immigrant to the United States, and almost all pastoring "dying" churches. As I sat there listening, I asked myself, why are we even bothering to get ordained if dying churches are the only ones we are sent to or called to serve? Having been in charge of such "dying" churches, I knew exactly what some of the women meant when they said they really couldn't afford to wait for people to come into their churches. Fran[2] said, "I have to go out and find them, and I really don't care who they are or where they are from. I am not concerned about making them Methodists, all I want is to share Jesus with them in their situations of need."

These are churches far from the core of what is considered healthy and viable, they are churches no one can really afford to pastor. However, for various reasons, none of which speak too well of the predominantly "white" mainline denominations, clergy from recent immigrant populations who choose to be ordained in these denominations land up taking charge or sent to these so called dying churches. In the midst of trying to understand

---

1 Andrew Walls, The Cross-Cultural Process in Christian History (Maryknoll: Orbis Books, 2002).

2 Name changed

what it means to be called or sent by Jesus to these "written off" churches in the margins, it dawned on me that I am focusing too much on a certain projected institutional clout as the core of doing church.

Despite the somewhat gloomy vignette, I was grateful for an opportunity afforded me by the Louisville Institute to embark on this particular study of recent immigrant women clergy and the impact of their presence in the mainline denominations of the American church. In addition to the insights I have gained into the complexities of church life, both at the congregational and institutional levels, this study has given me the opportunity to question and know myself better. I have found myself asking these questions:

- What does it mean for me to answer my call into ordained ministry in the Episcopal Church?
- How do people actually perceive my leadership and me?
- Am I really comfortable amongst the other?
- How am I being called to bring hard conversations to the table?
- Do I, as a recent immigrant, as a woman from the margins, really have a unique voice to bring to the church?

It has been reassuring to find the number of first generation immigrant women in ordained ministry who share my story of surmounting great obstacles before finally getting ordained. However, getting ordained has not necessarily meant more opportunities of "respectable" leadership in the larger church for many of these women. Given the vast number of recent immigrant populations from all over the world, I thought it best to narrow down my study to recent East Asian and South Asian immigrant women clergy in the mainline churches.

Since this project was done, I have had more interactions with women leaders of Asian descent serving as lay leaders both in mainline denominational churches as well as non-denominational churches. The leadership experiences of the women I have had the privilege to meet and listen to are varied; anywhere from "encouraged," "fulfilling," to "it's a struggle," and feeling "unrecognized." In the context of current socio-cultural conversations pertaining to Christian faith that have given rise to terms like Dones and Nones, I feel (as one representing the church), that I must be open to the possibility of a certain form of Christian expression within the institution of the Church that is being uncontrollably reshaped by forces beyond the "authority" of the institutional Church. Furthermore, by the time I revisited this study and expanded my conversation, the term "multicultural" churches has evolved in my consciousness to become "multiracial" churches, which I believe better captures the vision of the younger generation of churchgoers from very different racial backgrounds whose "American" identity and a shared ethos of inclusivity far overrides their "immigrant" or "cultural" identities. This was certainly the case for most newer non-denominational churches in the NYC area who identify themselves as "multiracial" rather than "multicultural."

Interviews:

Within the Episcopal Church, the west coast of the country has been better at recognizing the need for "multicultural" ministries. I, therefore, made a trip to the Episcopal Diocese of Los Angeles to interview the Suffragan Bishop of LA, who is in charge of multicultural ministries as well as some recent immigrant women clergy. Within The United Methodist Church, I interviewed two women clergy in New Jersey, and was also able to attend the biennial conference of the Asian American and Pacific Islander Clergywomen of The United Methodist Church in Claremont, California (Oct. 6-8, 2014). In the Presbyterian Church (USA), I interviewed one Chinese American clergywoman in New York. For this study, I interviewed seven Asian American women clergy from CA, NY, and NJ, also with the Rt. Rev. Diane M Jardine Bruce, Suffragan Bishop of LA (Episcopal), and the Rev. Dr. Christopher J Wright, International Ministries Director of Langham Partnership International, author of several books including, The Mission of God: Unlocking the Bible's Grand Narrative. Beyond these interviews, I had extensive conversations with more than a dozen Asian American women in church leadership—ordained as well as lay, both in the mainline denominations as well as non-denominational churches. Furthermore, I took a short survey of lay leaders in three churches on their experience with minority/immigrant women leadership in their churches: Grace Church, Millbrook, NY, All Angels' Church, NY, & Calvary-St. George's Church, NY.

The interviews with the seven clergywomen had some common stories of longer than normal process toward the ordained ministry; a longer and more difficult process of adjustment between said clergy and the congregations they were called into or sent to; a sense of being marginalized by the leadership of the larger church body; being paid less in comparison to their Anglo colleagues with equivalent educational qualifications and years of experience; lastly, most of them found themselves pastoring churches that were considered "dying." With all the difficulties faced by these women, I was deeply moved by their strong sense of call by God to His Church. Almost all of them spoke of an intentional engagement with those who are "unchurched" and had stories of reaching out to those who might not necessarily go looking for a church. The women shared honestly about the initial awkwardness of both "Anglo" parishioners and the newer immigrant parishioners with each other. They spoke of how the barriers of language and culture had to be negotiated carefully and wisely, how mistakes were made and are still being made. But in the end, they spoke of the rewarding experience of getting to a place of respect for each other and even to a place of shared leadership for various ministries. In terms of areas to address in the situation of a minority/immigrant woman going into a predominantly "Anglo" parish, I was surprised to find that many spoke of the whole congregations' need to go through an actual process of preparation to welcome an immigrant woman of color as their pastor and not just the clergy person.

The interview with the Rt. Rev. Diane M Jardine Bruce, Bishop Suffragan of the Episcopal Diocese of LA was, I thought, particularly helpful in understanding a certain form of racism involved in calling a woman of color, especially a relatively recent immigrant clergy person, as lead pastor or even as an associate/assistant pastor. One of the questions I asked Bishop Bruce was about the reluctance from other bishops to be engaged in multi-cultural ministries. Some of her observations were:

It is lack of openness…The other thing is—for some of the bishops, they view multicultural ministry as outreach not ministry… What ends up happening—the translation of that is that the clergy are paid less, the clergy are not honored at the same level. If you are a male ethnic clergy person you are paid less than your male counterpart, if you are a female ethnic clergy, you are paid the least of anybody on the totem pole. That's just the reality and it's a bad reality.

Personal Journey:

When I started on this project in February of 2014, I had just wrapped up my interim ministry with Grace Church in Millbrook, NY. Seeking another call, I applied to several churches in the Diocese where there were openings, including rectors' positions, associate clergy positions, interim pastor positions and priest-in-charge positions. For most of the positions I applied to, I made it to the final list of candidates; however, unfortunately for me, all the churches ended up calling others, all of whom as it turned out were white male or female clergy. I tried to see their decision as unrelated to my color, ethnicity or immigrant status. However, it was difficult not to recall the words of Bishop Diane Bruce: "Most of the Episcopal churches will not call you to be their priest, and this has got nothing to do with you. It is because they have never seen someone like you in leadership in their churches and they will just not take the risk."

When I brought up this particular insight from the Bishop with our Diocesan Canon for Transition Ministry, she was shocked. I would like to think that it is not a matter of racism in the strictest sense, but a matter of education, raising awareness and maybe to a large degree—fear of change to long held traditions.

For the last five years I have been involved in interim ministry, not so much out of choice but for lack of other opportunities. What I am learning through my engagement in interim ministry is that it does open an opportunity for a person like me to break down some of the barriers toward leadership for people of color that definitely exists in mainline churches, especially the Episcopal Church. Interim ministry is, by definition, not a long-term commitment, and this might be the reason why congregations may be more open to calling a person from a minority/immigrant population to fill such a leadership position. This could become a great opportunity for churches to experience the leadership of a person of color and engage in a more genuine conversation on diversity and inclusiveness.

As a part of this study, I got the opportunity to attend the biennial conference of the Asian American and Pacific Islander Clergywomen of The United Methodist Church (UMC) in 2014. The conference certainly gave the impression that the Methodist Church has been more intentional about moving toward creating multicultural churches. Just the fact that there is such an organization within the UMC of Asian American and Pacific Islander clergywomen tells me that they have been welcoming and maybe even recruiting women from immigrant populations much earlier than other mainline denominations. This particular hospitality toward the leadership of women from recent immigrant groups could possibly be driven by the fact that the traditionally "white" churches are bleeding members (giving rise to the term "Dones"). Nonetheless, it appears that the denomination has seized the opportunity to find more fertile ground for church growth amongst recent immigrant populations, which has necessitated raising clergy leadership from within such communities. The other factor to be considered for the presence of a larger number of clergy leadership from minority/immigrant populations could be the practice in the UMC of bishops appointing pastors to congregations making this denomination more attractive for women from minority/immigrant backgrounds to seek ordination with them.

Regardless of the reasons for the UMC's greater welcome toward immigrant women (and men) seeking ordination, the denomination as a whole seems to have made more progress in nurturing "multicultural" churches. A few of the recent immigrant women pastors of the UMC are senior pastors in some of their fastest growing, larger churches. These women clergy shared that within a few years of their arrival, they saw the demographics of their congregations change to reflect more racial and generational diversity. The few stories of "successful" ethnic pastors in multicultural churches by no means tell the whole story. The more common story by far is of deep struggle faced by women clergy in small churches trying to transform not only parishioners but also the very communities in which their churches are situated.

One book that has been helpful in my understanding of the complexities of racial relations in America and certainly found its way into the life of the church is, "A Different Mirror: A History of Multicultural America" by Ronald Takaki. Having read the book, it seems plausible that one way to see the reluctance of the mainline churches to embrace diversity in clergy leadership while giving lip service to inclusiveness stems from a misguided, and maybe a subconscious belief that to be American is to be white. It would be naïve to say that the notion of America as a "white" nation is merely about the color of one's skin. From the readings, I am inclined to say that it is much more about what is perceived and propagated as the "real" American way of life, which at the institutional level, including the mainline churches is overwhelmingly defined by a worldview of white Protestantism.[3] This particular worldview as embodied in the mainline churches values a certain sense of propriety or decorum over and against other equally valid but distinct expressions of Christianity. Experiencing worship in different congregations, I have to ask myself if the liturgy and hymnal of the Episcopal Church connects with the new immigrant worshipper? Bishop Bruce's immediate response, when I asked her this question was:

> The BCP (Book of Common Prayer) is flexible but we have got to make it more flexible so that we can be creative about it to meet the needs of the people that are coming through our doors. They might or might not speak English, and in fact they may speak English exactly like me, but their language is not the language of that prayer book... We have to learn what their heart language is.

---

3   Ronald Takaki, A Different Mirror: A History of Multicultural America (New York: Back Bay Books/Little, Brown and Company, 2008).

As much as I am appreciative of traditions, I do not believe any one tradition is superior to another. Moreover, even good traditions need to be revisited to see if they still carry the same depth of spiritual meaning to the current or prospective worshipers as it did for people many hundreds of years ago. Unfortunately, often, openness to liturgical diversity or innovation is seen as too risky a prospect, which in turn perpetuates the unhealthy environment of discouraging new contributions to the worship life of the church. This view of the church, where "tradition" (including liturgy, worship style, preaching style, church polity and leadership) more strongly defines the life of the church rather than the radical welcome message of the Gospel of Jesus Christ is, I believe, a significant factor that has led to the emergence of the Dones and the Nones within the American religious landscape.

Theologically, I hold a high view of the Body of Christ (the church) and "the priesthood of all believers." I have tried to understand Apostle Paul's metaphor of the importance of every member of the body (1 Corinthians 12) working together for the optimum health of the whole Body in the light of my own upbringing in a community oriented tribal society (Nagaland, India). As much as there are things that I don't agree with in the community that I grew up in, this much I have seen, that the sense of identity and connectedness to the community is an intentional process. It calls for collaborative work and the recognition of each generation's gift of wisdom and talents to renew and keep alive a body of very disparate individuals negotiating a fast changing world. My upbringing and exposure to conversations around the need for change in church leadership and the very notion of church in America give me hope that God is building up the church in a new way.

For many of the recent immigrant clergy (women in this case), it is not merely an intellectual exercise to engage in such conversations, it is the painstaking work of becoming malleable to very complex situations on the ground, where often the challenge is beyond preaching the redemptive and self-denying message of Jesus Christ. The greater challenge for these clergy is to reconcile, in their own lives, the Gospel message of radical welcome and dignity afforded to all of humanity, and especially the marginalized, with the blatant racism as well as sexism faced within the institutional church. Under such an environment, recent immigrant clergy have taken the initiative to reach out more intentionally to their own immigrant communities. It is no wonder that in the New York Metropolitan area, some of the fastest growing churches are what would be categorized as "immigrant" or "ethnic" churches or churches led by a person of color from a recent immigrant group (South Asians and Africans).

To look at the phenomenon of Dones and Nones only from a "white" church lens would be shortsighted and dismissive of the validity and the viability of the growing churches in recent immigrant communities. It could very well be that God is working in a new way amongst/through a new people as He has done time and time again. The influx of new people and new cultures will, I believe, bring with it new ideas of leadership as well as a new perception of authority forcing the existing Church in America to redefine the very notion of the Body of Christ, the notion of denominational divides and traditions, and finally the understanding of authority and leadership, which is already happening in places where courageous women (and men) from recent immigrant communities have answered the call to be the prophetic presence in the American church landscape, which seems to be dotted with collapsing buildings, fleeing Dones and indifferent Nones.

Nonetheless, robust immigrant churches are not necessarily the answer to reviving the fast declining mainline churches. As I have gotten acquainted with a few para-church organizations that are involved largely with Asian congregations, I have come to see that for many of these immigrant/ethnic churches, vestiges of the nineteenth century missionary movements from the Western world to the East have been brought back to the West by immigrants, which unfortunately are still dictating their theology as well as their worship and leadership styles. At a recent women's conference organized by the group—Women of Wonder! based out of New York City engaged primarily with immigrant churches, the question came up about whether it is within God's will to leave a church where there is no encouragement or affirmation of women in church leadership. Currently, even with such struggles toward a more equal platform for both men and women in church leadership, the women continue to stay in the more fundamentalist immigrant church, rather than finding a more progressive church. However, if the issue of women's rightful place in church leadership and authority is not addressed soon, even these thriving immigrant churches will begin to see a significantly large number of the Dones and Nones emerge from their communities. It would also be prudent to take into account that this sense of an outdated and clearly discriminatory model of church leadership is felt not just by women but by a majority of the younger generation amongst the immigrant communities. For the moment, those who feel discriminated against still continue to stay in these churches, because, for better or worse, these "immigrant" churches do seem to inculcate a strong sense of belonging to the community, fostered by a shared cultural heritage.

As case studies of how racial diversity in leadership promotes uncommon growth in a church, by which I mean more than numerical growth, I have looked at two of the most diverse and vibrant churches in New York City—All Angels' Church (Episcopal), and New Life Fellowship Church (non-denominational). Both churches have significant ministry to the homeless (All Angels' church) and to the immigrant and minority communities (New Life Fellowship). The multiracial leadership in both the churches may be one of the strong factors in raising awareness of the needs in marginalized communities that has led to their engagement in not just "meeting needs" but more importantly empowering and assimilating the poor and the powerless into their worshiping communities. The diversity of race/ethnicity and economic backgrounds as well as gender equality in leadership are what draws the "missing" generation to these churches.

On leadership staff at All Angels' Church are: 1. Rector—The Rev. Milind Sojwal (South Asian American), who also happens to be my husband (so I could be biased, but there are enough positive testimonies that would corroborate my observation of growth and vitality in the church over the last sixteen years he has been Rector); 2. Vicar—The Rev. Christine Lee (Korean American); 3. Interim Director of Worship Arts—Dr. Peter McCulloch (White American); 4. Director of Community Ministries—Chelsea Horvath (White American); 6. Director for Children and Family ministries—Mary Ellen Lehman (White American); 7. Coordinators for Youth Ministry—Kegan Smallwood and Trevor St. John-Gilbert (both White American); others hailing from African American, Hispanic and various Asian backgrounds are also actively engaged as lay leaders.[4] Parishioners from both minority and "white" populations have said that they were attracted to All Angels' Church because of the diversity in leadership, a strong sense of community, an intentional hospitality toward the homeless that incorporates them into the church community beyond a "feeding program," and the "non-traditional" worship that still retains all elements of an Anglican liturgy. In a denomination where the average age of parishioners is in the mid 60s, the average age at All Angels' Church is in the 20s. Sixteen years ago, when Milind was interviewed for the Rectors' position at All Angels' Church, the then Bishop of the Diocese emphatically told the search committee that they could not call him as Rector because he is not American, by which he probably meant "white." The head of the search committee refused to accept the Bishop's directive and finally the Bishop relented. Today, All Angels' Church is the only church in the diocese in conversation with the Bishop to find them a larger worship space.

The New Life Fellowship church, in Queens, NY, is one of the fastest growing non-denominational multi-racial churches in NYC. It has members from more than seventy-three countries and has a very significant membership of millennials. On their ministry leadership team are: 1. Pastor of Worship Ministries—Cate Song (Asian American); 2. Community Life Resident—Edward Dhanpat Jr. (Guyanese American); 3. Marriage Ministry/Pastor at Large—Geri Scazzero (White American); 4. Sunday Connections Coordinator—Jessica Rechner (White American); 5. Leader in Residence—Joseph Terry (Puerto Rican/African American); 6. Assistant Kids Ministry Director—Kelly Fol (White American); 7. Youth Pastor—Matthew Manno (Italian/African American); 8. Community Life Coordinator—Myrna Rohdin (Hispanic American); 9. Executive Pastor of Communities—Peter Rohdin (White American); 10. Founder/Teaching Pastor at large—Pete Scazzero (White American); 11. Executive Director of New Life Fellowship and New Life CDC—A. Redd Sevilla (Asian American); 12. Lead Pastor—Rich Villadas (Puerto Rican American); 13. Kids Ministry Director—Sosangela Villados (Puerto Rican American);

---

4   "All Angels' Church," Accessed December 10, 2016,
http://www.allangelschurch.com/about-us/staff

14. Executive Director of Emotionally Healthy Spirituality—Ruth Zsolnai (Puerto Rican).[5]

From the various resources I have been able to gather, the rise of Christian leadership from amongst immigrant populations is happening rapidly here in America. However, due to the lack of enthusiasm to embrace emerging leaders from minority populations in the mainline churches, these leaders are finding other avenues to minister in non-denominational churches as well as non-profit organizations that affirm and celebrate diversity in leadership. According to an article in Christianity today (October, 2014 issue), titled: "Asian Americans: Silent No More"

> It's still possible to miss the ways Asian Americans are shaping American Christianity. With just a few exceptions, Asian Americans rarely headline major conferences, attract media attention, or top Christian publishing's bestseller list. But thanks to their bicultural heritage and the particular challenges it brings, Asian American Christians are finding they have unique voices and gifts that allow them to connect with both non-Asian American audiences and segments of the church that no one else can reach.[6]

My hope is that a study like this is just the beginning of the conversation toward a more inclusive practice for leadership in the mainline churches; not only as a matter of non-discrimination and survival, but more importantly as a matter of obedience to God's call into His ever-expanding colorful Kingdom. As much as the stories on the ground would like to dictate, I do not want this study to be about the conscious or unconscious resistance of the mainline churches toward people of color for important leadership/decision making positions. I would rather we draw our attention to the need for multiracial leadership to be embraced and encouraged in the mainline churches if we are to reflect the rapidly changing population and culture of America, or should I say, reflect the true image of God that

---

5   "New Life Fellowship," Accessed December 10, 2016,
http://newlifefellowship.org/about-us/about-new-life/our-staff/

6   Helen Lee, "Asian Americans: Silent No More," Christianity Today 58 (2014): 38-43.

transcends all racial categories. In choosing to be gatekeepers of sharply declining churches, the mainline denominations may exclude themselves from participating in the dynamic movement of the Holy Spirit that is happening in a new way within and beyond their doors.

All this is not to say that the mainline churches are bad or doomed while emerging independent churches are good and growing. There is much to learn from each other and this is, in fact, I feel, the best time and maybe currently, the best country to rally together as faith companions belonging to the same Body of Christ, wherein, we can enrich our understanding of what it means to be the beloved Community of Christ. I believe that leadership, which transforms a community must be counter-cultural (church culture in this case), and for it to be genuine it must necessarily arise from a particular situational need. In other words, transformational leadership in essence is an unconventional organic response to a crisis.

Many of the recent immigrant clergywomen I met, in practice, are being pushed into churches that are in crisis. Under such situations, the need for transformational leadership from the clergy is not a matter of training but a matter of survival and, ultimately, new life. If the clergy in such churches are given the kind of support and encouragement they need at this crucial time, these churches in the margins may have the opportunity to become vibrant congregations with significant changes in demographics, liturgy, music and, more importantly, leadership of both lay and ordained. However, there should be dire concern for the future if this particular pattern of sending clergywomen (or men) from minority/immigrant populations into "dying" churches continues. Under such discriminatory practices, it is unlikely that younger people and people of color will seek ordination or leadership of any kind in the mainline denominations. There is a growing consciousness among young people of minority populations about their significance and their contributions and influence in the larger society. So why would they come to serve in places where they are patronized and perceived as less than their white counterparts?

I believe we have come to the moment, which Andrew F. Walls calls the "Ephesian moment" when the West experiences a diversity in the Christian population as never seen before and with it the emergence of an ecclesiology that is very different from what the West is used to. In order for us to participate in this very important moment in the Church's life, I would like to see crucial conversations in the mainline churches happen about the need for multicultural leadership that includes everyone, especially those who currently hold most of the ecclesiastical power. As long as conferences and dialogues about raising and nurturing multi-cultural leadership in the Church happen only within a certain subgroup of people, say, Asian American, Pacific Islander, African American, or Hispanic, the tone of the conversations may continue to sound like mere grievances and the gatherings more like support groups. For real openness toward more diversity in church leadership, conversations need to happen not just at the institutional level but also at the parish level. These conversations must be accompanied by the proactive recruitment and the creation of better and/ or equal opportunities of leadership for clergy from minority/immigrant populations in the mainline churches. All this does not mean that the fast dwindling membership of the mainline churches can be reversed soon; in all probability, God is doing something new that may very well mean the demise of the Church that has long harbored the "most segregated hour" (The Rev. Dr. Martin Luther King Jr.) in America.

The hope for Christianity in America should not center around the formal gatherings of like-minded people in a designated place of worship—following an order of worship that is no longer of the people, for the people. The spiritual ground is indeed shifting and as believers of a God who has become incarnate amongst us, we join in the Anglican Collect pronounced at The Ordination of a Priest:

O God of unchangeable power and eternal light: Look favorably on your whole church, that wonderful and sacred mystery; by the effectual working of your providence, carry out in tranquility the plan of salvation; let the whole world see and know that things which were cast down are being raised up, and things which had grown old are being made new, and that all things are being brought to their perfection by him through whom all things were made. Your Son Jesus Christ our Lord;

who lives and reigns with you, in the unity of the Holy Spirit, one God, for ever and ever. Amen. (The Book of Common Prayer).[7]

---

7   Episcopal Church, The Book of Common Prayer and Administration of the Sacraments and other Rites and Ceremonies of the Church: Together with the Psalter or Psalms of David according to the use of the Episcopal Church (New York: Seabury Press, 1979).

↓

Book Reviews

At Home In Exile: Finding Jesus Among My Ancestors And Refugee Neighbors

Russell Jeung (Grand Rapids, MI: Zondervan Press, 2016)

Reviewed by Jerry Park
Baylor University

Sociologist Russell Jeung is an academic hero to many. At times I have often wondered what his life experiences must have been like to retain his reputation as a scholar teacher, social activist and community organizer, motivated by a personal faith. In this memoir Jeung steps away from his professional identity and academic tone in favor of his religious and ethnic identities that many will find interesting and engaging.

Jeung's experiences and family life pull together in ways that may be familiar to many evangelical Asian American readers. Attending a prestigious undergraduate institution (Stanford), teaching English overseas, joining a Christian collective residing side-by-side with southeast Asians and Latinos, and obtaining a PhD (Berkeley) serve as one strand among several that indicate his awareness of the Asian American model minority stereotype and the radical communalism sometimes heard of in evangelical circles. Unlike most highly educated Christian Asian Americans however he responded to the call to live radically in a way that secular progressives and middle-class evangelicals may find startling. His life experiences, as familiar as they are to so many second-generation Asian Americans are balanced with the less familiar experience of being a multigenerational descendant of Chinese Americans whose origins in the US date back to the beginning of the 20th century. Jeung effectively employs his understanding of his family's struggles and their specific origins as Hakka ("guest people"), a Chinese ethnic people who have experienced repeated displacement. For the Hakka who arrived in the US, opportunities for upward mobility were often undercut by the deliberate structural racism reminiscent of African Americans in the Jim Crow south. Jeung traces his (and consequently our ...) personal call to social justice from the marginalization experienced in his family tree starting from the early 20th century to the privilege he rests upon as a result of their communal self-empowerment motivated by persistent Chinese and Christian sensibilities

Jeung introduces us to a number of Chinese terms (rooted in Confucianism) that reflect certain Christian themes of community and the call to suffer with the marginalized and leverage power and privilege on their behalf. For Jeung and his fellow Berkeley-trained Christian compatriots it was their education and network connections that resulted in helping numerous refugees and undocumented immigrants in the dilapidated complex of the Oak Park Apartments.

It's telling that Jeung's use of his Chinese heritage, with its many Confucian inflections offers a rehabilitative view of this ethic that in Korean American Protestant communities is often a source of persistent intraethnic inequality. Where Korean Protestantism's Confucian influence seems to oppress women, alienate the second-generation, and generate intense status anxiety leading to conflict, schism and undiagnosed psychological trauma, Jeung's utilization of Confucianism invites readers to see interconnectedness and interdependence, as well as food and sacrifice as elements in which one can build an ethnic-infused Christian identity that builds cross-class and cross-racial ties. One wonders why Jeung's understanding is infrequently invoked relative to other renderings.

Jeung's memoir reflects a "usable past" wherein personal moments in his family's history gain purchase in one's life today. It is in some ways an attempt to emulate African American Protestants who can trace a collective and robust history of resistance and uplift through churches. But Asian American Protestants face a major demographic complication that may make the development of a usable past difficult. Most Americans who identify as Black can trace their roots back multiple generations; immigrant Blacks are in the minority. By contrast, a small fraction of Asian Americans like Jeung have such roots; the majority are immigrants largely arriving after 1965 or their children. This results in a very short "relevant" history for many Asian Americans who want to trace a personal familial line the way Jeung has done.

Jeung sprinkles his narrative with Christian Bible verses which may come across to some as theologically unsophisticated (for the well-read armchair Christian theologian) or alienating (for the social activist religious skeptic). These instances came as a surprise to me given the non-sectarian tone Jeung's social science research often demands. Jeung writes to an audience that is motivated in part by consistency with the Christian scriptures and while he identifies as an evangelical, his use of texts that focus on social justice and the prophets reveal his extensive reading and knowledge of the canon.

At Home in Exile is an excellent memoir, and one that Asian American Christians (and their non-Asian American fellow believers) will find engaging, entertaining and perhaps inspiring to those seeking a way to make their ethnic and Christian identities cohere in a more consistent way toward bringing about shalom in an unequal society.

Jerry Park

is an associate professor of sociology at Baylor university. His research is focused on religion, race relations, civic engagement with a focus on Asian Americans.

Asian American Christian Ethics: Voices, Methods, Issues

Grace Y. Kao and Ilsup Ahn, eds. (Waco, Tex.: Baylor University Press, 2015)

Reviewed by Amos Yong
Fuller Theological Seminary, Pasadena, CA

The genesis of this volume derives from the Asian and Asian American Working Group of the Society for Christian Ethics. The twelve contributors are all Asians or Asian American ethicists and/or academics across a range of theological disciplines, and they address in this book eleven important topics in Christian ethics: 1) gender and sexuality, 2) marriage, family, and parenting, 3) virtue ethics, 4) peace and war, 5) wealth and prosperity, 6) racial identity and solidarity, 7) health care, 8) immigration, 9) the environment, 10) education and labor, and 11) cosmetic surgery. The volume editors have also included an informative introductory chapter and a very brief concluding reflection.

This reviewer deeply appreciates the methodology employed across the book. In each of the eleven cases, the authors first provide an overview of historic Christian ethical reflection on the topic at hand or at least situate the topic in the contemporary socio-historical and theological landscape. Second, thick descriptions of Asian American realities in relationship to the topic are laid out. The third and final section includes in almost all cases theological reflection that engages Asian American concerns with Christian ethical perspectives. As an Asian American myself, I was encouraged to see that the Asian American in the volume title was clearly delineated and excavated throughout, never in an essentialized manner but always in the relevant historic, phenomenological, and social terms in the second sections but then also effectively interwoven into the final reflections. As a scholar with interest but not expertise in Christian ethics, the initial sections of each chapter enabled appreciation of the broader discursive field amidst which my colleagues are engaging the issues. Finally, as a Christian theologian, I found myself consistently and pleasantly surprised by the depth of the theological reflection found across these pages. The Christian in the title of the book is also meaningful and weighty, especially insofar as almost all of the chapters attempt to formulate a creative and constructive Asian American response that is not devoid of substantive theological considerations. This is not to say that each of the eleven chapters in the body of the volume is equally robust across these three major sections. It is to say that the there is a consistency from chapter to chapter that reflects both clear conceptualization of the framework of the book and its parts, and commitment by the contributors to adhere to the (presumably) agreed-upon format. Obviously the editors are to be thanked for ensuring structural conformity from case to case, but the result is an exceedingly invaluable book for students – not only graduate but also undergraduate – of Christian ethics in general but also of Asian American perspective on these ethical issues.

There is very little to criticize in a volume that is supposed to open up avenues for Asian American thinking about Christian ethics and the book reads, by and large, as initiating conversation rather than as proposing any final word on the challenges at hand. My own suspicions are that the concerns to avoid essentializing Asian American identity or viewpoints may have inhibited more robust consideration of at least some of the issues in dialogue with historically Asian resources. When these latter appear, they function descriptively rather than normatively (i.e., philosophically or ethically). From a Christian theological vantage point, many Asian Americans, especially those from more conservative Protestant traditions, would embrace the specifically Christian character of the directions charted as not being synthesized (or "syncretized") with particularly Asian religious traditions. Yet globalization and transnational dynamics will only intensify in the present century so that the lines between Asia and America will continue to blur. Along these trajectories, not only Asian Americans but also all Christians, including Christian ethicists, will not be able to ignore how Asian wisdom traditions will continue to impinge upon, if not also be able to resource, Christian reflection in global context. So let me conclude that Asian American Christian Ethics ought to be read as precipitating inter- and trans-continental dialogue and discussion so that Asian American Christian thought can be enriched by, as well as inform, other Asian religious, cultural, and philosophical engagements with ethics for the next generation of global citizens.

Amos Yong

 is Professor of Theology & Mission, and director of the Center for Missiological Research at Fuller Theological Seminary; he is the author or editor of almost four dozen books.